Champions on Ice

TOM COLLINS presents

Champions

on Ice

CHRISTINE BRENNAN

FOREWORD BY BRIAN BOITANO

To the lady in the blue skates

– C.B.

National Library of Canada Cataloguing in Publication

Brennan, Christine
    Champions on Ice : twenty-five years of the world's finest figure skaters / Christine Brennan.

Includes index.
ISBN 0-7710-1648-4

1. Champions on Ice. 2. Skaters. 3. Skating. I. Title.

GV850.55.C48B74 2002   796.91'2   C2002 903943-6

Published simultaneously in the United States of America by McClelland & Stewart Ltd.,
P.O. Box 1030, Plattsburgh, New York 12901.

Library of Congress Control Number: 2002110987

We acknowledge the financial support of the Government of Canada through the Book Publishing Industry Development Program for our publishing activities. We further acknowledge the support of the Canada Council for the Arts and the Ontario Arts Council for our publishing program.

Typeset in Fairfield, Gill Sans and Univers by PageWave Graphics Inc., Toronto

Digital color separation by Embassy Stafford, Toronto

Printed and bound in Canada

McClelland & Stewart Ltd.
The Canadian Publishers
481 University Avenue
Toronto, Ontario
M5G 2E9
www.mcclelland.com

1 2 3 4 5   06 05 04 03 02

Contents

Foreword

"*I* MADE IT, I finally made it!" I thought to myself. I had just made THE TOUR. I was 17, and I had been asked to skate on the tour of Olympic and world figure skating champions. It was the most prestigious and the most successful skating tour in the history of the sport, and I was about to begin what would consume a large part of my adult life, skating in 18 different Champions on Ice tours.

From a skater's perspective, Tom Collins' Champions on Ice is *the* tour to be on. Skaters want to skate for Tom. Having been a skater himself, Tom understood what it took to perform night after night, and so he produced a touring show where the only thing the skaters had to worry about was their skating. All the travel arrangements and meals before and after the show were taken care of by the management. Skaters could even do their laundry backstage. As the tours became longer, workout equipment and weights appeared backstage, and a trainer was added to the staff. For young up-and-coming skaters, the money they earned on the tour provided a chance to defray the cost of training expenses, and it was a chance to perform without being judged. And for every skater, it meant being part of a very select group. Friendships were made that broke the barrier between East and West long before the Cold War was over. It was and still is a tight-knit fraternity, crafted out of shared experiences on the road.

From an audience perspective and a historical perspective, Champions on Ice is *the* tour to see. It is the only place you can see all the best in the world in one show, where the top professionals perform alongside the current amateur champions. Every Olympic gold medalist in figure skating since 1972 has appeared in Champions on Ice. The tour's star-studded casts hastened the demise of the single-star-driven production as spectators became used to seeing all their favorite skaters live under one roof. And Champions on Ice introduced the exhibition-style tour, where for the first time audiences could see the skaters demonstrate their own distinct on-ice personalities away from competitive restraints.

And the man behind the tour? That's Tom Collins, affectionately known as Tommy. He is the only person to have been inducted into the U.S., Canadian and world figure skating halls of fame. Tom Collins is a man of endless energy who has devoted his life to Champions on Ice. He stands unique in the tough business of promotion, a man of loyalty and vision… with the soul of a skater.

— Brian Boitano

The Tour Begins

"**F**IVE MINUTES!"

The voice echoed through the dressing rooms, pushing the figure skaters toward the ice for the very first moments of what would become the longest tour in the history of Champions on Ice — and, for that matter, the longest tour in the annals of figure skating.

"Five minutes, everyone!"

Out they came, hurriedly trudging along in their glittering costumes and their skate guards, shaking an arm or a leg to try to remove the cobwebs of the Olympic season. As an audience of thousands sat in the stands, the skaters gathered in darkness in a tunnel leading to the ice and waited.

There was Michelle Kwan, who had grown up on the tour looking up to her mentor, Brian Boitano, now taking his place as the audience's most-beloved skater. There was Sarah Hughes, earnestly filling the role of the tour's newest superstar, and Timothy Goebel, finding his footing as America's leading man.

Where they now stood, Peggy Fleming, Dorothy Hamill, Scott Hamilton, Tai Babilonia, Randy Gardner, Ekaterina Gordeeva and Sergei Grinkov had been once before.

"Tommy Collins' is the only tour to ever have had every star," Boitano said. "No other tour can say that. You name a star, they've been on Tommy's tour. I mean, he's had everybody. If you put together a list of all the people who've ever been on his tour, it's huge."

Showtime: Michelle Kwan is about to step onto the ice to start the 2002 Champions on Ice tour.

The husband-and-wife ice dance team of Jerod Swallow and Liz Punsalan joined the tour in 1994, and two years later, they found themselves working beside Hamill, their childhood hero.

"We grew up watching Dorothy win the gold medal in 1976," Swallow said. "That's my first Olympic memory. I was 10. And then to eventually be touring with her, standing next to her in an ensemble…"

"You were holding her hand as part of the number," Punsalan reminded him.

"Yeah," Swallow said, smiling.

"It's almost like Tommy Collins is a dream-maker," Boitano said. "When you're a kid, you think to your-self, 'God, if I could just make it on that tour.' And when you make it on that tour, it's just like a dream come true. It's a moment when you feel, 'I've made it. I have finally made it. I am someone in the skating world because I am on this tour.' It's the only time other than winning a national championship or a world title or an Olympic medal that you feel that way."

$\mathcal{F}$OUR DAYS EARLIER, another voice had called them together, piercing the darkness in the arena.

"Hello, hello!"

The voice echoed through what was then an empty building.

"Welcome, everyone!"

Everyone? How about anyone? It was noon on the Saturday of Easter Weekend, 2002, and only two soli-tary skaters, Elvis Stojko and Michael Weiss, were making circles on the crusty Florida ice at the Ocean Center in Daytona Beach.

Everyone might have been welcomed, but most of Weiss and Stojko's peers were nowhere to be found.

It was time to start the first practice session for the 93-show, 85-city tour of Champions on Ice, and choreographer Sarah Kawahara definitely needed to locate a few more figure skaters.

"The sooner we get going," she said across the public address system, "the faster we get to the beach."

That did it. One minute into the new tour, and already it was time for a little bribery.

On a holiday weekend, with the Atlantic Ocean one block away and 80-degree warmth and sunshine just outside the arena door, Kawahara found the perfect way to entice a collection of weary, travel-worn

skaters onto the ice. Goebel took Kwan's hand to help her as she stepped through the opening in the boards, pulling off her skate guards to begin her ninth year on tour. Nicole Bobek and Liz Punsalan came trudging along the carpet from backstage, followed by Peter Tchernyshev and Jerod Swallow. Soon, Kawahara and her creative sidekick Brian Klavano, the tour's performance director, had more than a dozen skaters assembled in front of them, including Viktor Petrenko, Philippe Candeloro, Surya Bonaly, Shae-Lynn Bourne and Victor Kraatz.

The first opportunity for Sarah Hughes (opposite) to skate as Olympic champion came on the 2002 tour. She went to high school during the week and joined the tour on weekends. Sarah Kawahara (above) choreographed the show's opening and closing numbers.

Kawahara and Klavano looked at the skaters, some of whom had just finished an Olympic season that had been as exhausting as it was rewarding.

The skaters stared right back, waiting for Kawahara and Klavano to say something that would magically transform them from a group of fiercely independent individuals into one cohesive unit.

This was the skating equivalent of the first day of school, except for the fact that many of them were not bright-eyed and bushy-tailed but just plain old bushed, running on empty after bouncing around the globe, from Salt Lake City to Nagano and back to America, chasing their dreams.

"Olympic stallions in their prime," Klavano thought with a wry smile.

Kawahara was thinking something else.

"They're fried."

True, but there was no time for excuses. Not with four days to go until the start of Tom Collins' 24th rendition of Champions on Ice.

No, there was no time to waste.

••

From teamwork to individuality: The first brushstrokes of the closing number were made under the direction of Brian Klavano (below). The change-of-edge spiral has been Michelle Kwan's trademark since 1997 (opposite).

SOON, QUEEN'S "We Are the Champions" was blaring over the public address, and the skaters were dancing free-form as Kawahara and Klavano conferred about who to put where in the group numbers. They had planned it out on notepads in Kawahara's dining room in the Los Angeles suburbs, then tried it out themselves in nearby rinks. But nothing completely resembled being there with the skaters, finally implementing the ideas with the performers themselves.

In addition to the 21 individual numbers performed each night, the tour needed an opening and a closing group number. Over the years, the opening and the finale had become more elaborate, which was why the skaters gave up Easter Weekend to spend four days preparing for the Olympic tour.

"It's like a Rubik's cube," Kawahara said. "So many people come and go throughout the tour that it gets really tricky. You take this one out, this one shifts. And to do it in three or four days? That's a tall order. People who are Olympic or world champions train a whole year for what they do. And then, all of a sudden, we do this in three or four days."

The process began nine months earlier with a meeting of the minds, including tour founder and executive producer Tom Collins, in Los Angeles. All the tour's creative people were there, including costume designer Pete Menefee and lighting director Marilyn Lowey. They began tossing around ideas; then, in the following weeks, Kawahara and Klavano plotted and planned how the numbers would look. For the opening, there would be cut after cut of popular music, each introducing a different skater, from "All Star" to "Here Comes the Sun" to "The World's Greatest."

And for the finale? They chose a big-band swing theme, something different, something new.

It was all set — until September 11.

• •

Elvis Stojko, a tour veteran, enjoys pushing the envelope with his unique individual numbers. You won't see this in the Olympics: Shae-Lynn Bourne and Victor Kraatz perform as a spider weaving a web.

"Tommy called in October and said, 'We really should be doing something patriotic,'" Kawahara said.

So they called another meeting. Kawahara was in the throes of preparing the massive skating productions for the Opening and Closing Ceremonies of the Salt Lake City Olympics, but she put together a demo tape of Jimi Hendrix playing "The Star-Spangled Banner" on guitar, followed by Ray Charles singing "America the Beautiful," then the Mormon Tabernacle Choir singing the "Battle Hymn of the Republic."

She played it for Collins in a hotel room in Los Angeles. He needed to hear it only once and he was sold. The finale would be nothing but red, white and blue — with Fourth of July fireworks every night. An all-American celebration borne from the minds of Canadians.

"I'm Canadian," Kawahara said. "Tom's Canadian. Brian's Canadian. But it was great because we live in the United States, we love it here, we are raising our families here. So we have Russian skaters and French skaters and Canadian skaters all being a part of this patriotic finale. But that's another great aspect of the tour, bringing different cultures together as one."

Alexei Yagudin (above) won the Olympic gold medal with two stirring performances in Salt Lake City, then joined the tour in the spring. Sasha Cohen (right), one of the stars of U.S. skating in 2002, performed "Hernando's Hideaway" on tour. The tour's finale (overleaf) was a red, white and blue international tribute to America.

$\mathcal{F}$ROM ITS EARLIEST DAYS as a small traveling troupe stopping in a few cities after the Olympics or a North American world championships, Champions on Ice had grown to become the touring manifestation of figure skating in the past two decades.

With the explosion of interest in figure skating after the Tonya Harding/Nancy Kerrigan saga of 1994, there now was much more money to be made on the tour. There were more teenaged skaters trying to make that money. And, among the fans and the media, there was far more interest in what skaters were doing year-round, not just during the competitive season.

This particular year, 2002, had seen more than its share of scandal, starting at the Olympic Games and continuing into the summer with allegations of Russian mafia influence on the Olympic results. Although Canadians Jamie Sale and David Pelletier and Russians Elena Berezhnaya and Anton Sikharulidze — the two pairs involved in the Olympic controversy — were not on the tour after the Games, both pairs had appeared in previous years. And French ice dancers Marina Anissina and Gwendal Peizerat would join the 2002 Champions on Ice tour not at the beginning but later in the year; they would leave before their names would be linked by U.S. investigators to the serious allegations of Russian mob involvement in the Salt Lake City Games.

But no matter how bad the news might get for figure skating, the sport (and Champions on Ice) also thrived on the public interest in its superstars, most notably the current Olympic medalists and world champions.

Singles skater Nicole Bobek (opposite) has become a mainstay as a professional with Champions on Ice. Russian Olympic gold medalists Oksana Kazakova and Artur Dmitriev (below) were up to their usual innovative tricks on tour.

"We could have danced all night:" Naomi Lang and Peter Tchernyshev (above) are four-time U.S. national champions. Liz Punsalan and Jerod Swallow (right) are five-time U.S. national champions. Marina Anissina and Gwendal Peizerat of France (opposite) won the 2002 Olympic gold medal.

FOUR WORLD TITLES MET one world title in the women's practices after the group sessions each day in Florida. Putting names with resumes, that would be Michelle Kwan and Irina Slutskaya, friends and competitors since 1994.

"This is very different from a competition," Kwan said. "In the locker room at a competition, we don't talk very much. Everyone is uptight, wired. This is the exact opposite. It's more approachable, carefree. You slowly get used to it."

Just one week earlier, Slutskaya had defeated Kwan in Nagano for her first world title. Little more than a month before that, both had lost to Sarah Hughes in one of the most surprising upsets in Olympic figure skating history.

Now they were on the same team of sorts, traveling together and working toward the same goal for the next four months. And, of all things, they were joined by Hughes and Sasha Cohen, giving the tour a murderers' row of talented women.

"When you're practicing together with the girls," Slutskaya said, "of course I'm looking at what they're doing and I think they're looking at what I'm doing."

Indeed they were. Kwan had put a triple lutz, the most difficult jump women do, in her "Fields of Gold" program. Slutskaya wasn't doing a lutz in her "Cotton-Eyed Joe" cowgirl number, in which she was dressed in full Western regalia, topped by a cowboy hat.

"It's hard for Irina," Kwan said. "She's got that hat on. How does she do that? I couldn't see with a baseball hat. How the heck does she land a triple with a hat on?"

Irina smiled. "It's not easy." Early in the tour, she experimented with all kinds of variations — hat on, hat off, hat sitting in the middle of the ice — before the hat was misplaced between tour stops in early June and disappeared entirely. Irina tried two other hats but they didn't fit, so she went hatless the rest of the tour.

••

Irina Slutskaya (opposite) has turned into a cowgirl in "Cotton-Eyed Joe." Olympic bronze medalist Tim Goebel (below), skated to Paul McCartney's "Spinning on an Axis" and "Freedom."

Ukrainian acrobats Oleksiy
Polishchuk and Vladimir Besedin
(above) become the most unusual
ballerinas to ever perform *Swan
Lake*. Tom Collins asked Rudy
Galindo (right) for a reprise of
"In the Navy" for the 2002 tour.
Michael Weiss (opposite) brought
to the tour a special pair of skates
with blades curved toward his heels.

But Kwan and Slutskaya were not the only women on the ice. They were joined by the tour's rapidly emerging younger generation, led by Hughes and Cohen. As Hughes unveiled a new program for the tour, put together in the hectic weeks between the Olympics and Daytona Beach, Kwan watched intently. This was Hughes' "I'll Never Say Goodbye" number, sung by Maureen McGovern. The song had special meaning for Hughes, who had been peppered with numerous questions about whether she would leave eligible skating for show-style skating like Olympic gold medalists Oksana Baiul and Tara Lipinski before her.

This was her answer, at least for the upcoming season.

The practice sessions those first four days before the tour began went from the sublime to the ridiculous. Viktor Petrenko loves to perform the preposterous program. The tour and its audiences know it and have come to expect it.

So it came as no surprise that he showed up for his practice session with a dog puppet attached to his arm, skating to the overwhelming "Who Let the Dogs Out."

In the stands watching was Estella Kwan, Michelle's mother and one of the mainstays of the tour's travel party. Estella was keeping an eye on Michelle's new traveling companion, a part-Maltese, part-poodle named Tofu.

Tofu was napping in a travel case no bigger than a purse beside Estella in the bleachers when Petrenko's music filled the arena. The moment Tofu heard the barking on the recording, she woke up and excitedly poked her head out of the opening of the case, believing she had found a friend. When she realized no other dogs were actually nearby, she quietly disappeared inside the case and went right back to sleep.

As the skaters learned the steps and footwork of the group numbers and worked on their own exhibition routines, they never forgot where they were. This was Florida, which meant those four days were definitely not filled with all work and no play.

During breaks that were too short to go back to the hotel but too long to stay inside the frigid arena, the skaters often wandered out to the loading dock, where they staked out their turf to do their second-favorite thing in the world besides skate: talk on their cell phones.

On the afternoon of the first show, April 3, 2002, Kwan sought outdoor refuge on top of a few of the tour's blue cases, stacked against the arena's outside wall. Slutskaya popped out of the loading dock door and picked a small patch of grass by the tour buses. She then dialed Moscow.

A few moments later, Hughes followed. She looked around. There was no more room on the grass, and Kwan had the cases all to herself.

So Hughes softly sat down on the concrete in the middle of the driveway and put her phone to her ear.

She may have won the Olympic gold medal, but she definitely lost this turf war.

Viktor Petrenko (opposite) performs with a canine friend to "Who Let the Dogs Out."

"Hello, hello:" Irina, Michelle and Sarah chat on their cell phones.

THE BLEACHERS BEGAN FILLING at 6:15 P.M. on Wednesday, April 3. As show time neared, the call came: "Five minutes!" The skaters began lining up in the tunnel that led to the ice. At the same time, just before the skaters charged out for the first official moments of the 24th Champions on Ice tour, Marty Collins, the tour coordinator, found his father by the zamboni. It was Tom Collins' birthday, and while one might expect it to be a day of great celebration, it was not. In fact, if the birthday was discussed at all, it was mentioned in a whisper backstage, because if there was one thing Tom Collins didn't want, it was attention paid to his birthday.

Marty, Tom's youngest son, handed his father a shopping bag. Inside was a card and a bottle of cologne.

"Thank you very much," Tom Collins said sarcastically. "I see you spent a lot of money on this."

Marty laughed. Giving each other the business: this was the Collins way.

Father and son walked toward the ice together to watch the show begin. First out, longtime Canadian pair Isabelle Brasseur and Lloyd Eisler. As they stepped through the boards, they squeezed each other's hands.

"Just relax," he said to her.

"Let's enjoy it," she said to him.

And off they went.

....

For the third time in their 13 years on tour, Isabelle Brasseur and Lloyd Eisler (below left) performed a gender-reversal number.
Dan Hollander (below right) draws laughter as Mrs. Doubtfire. Irina Grigorian (opposite) typifies Tom Collins' quest for novelty in a skating show.

Here's a surprise: Philippe Candeloro (opposite) is skating without his shirt. Surya Bonaly (left) has the extension and reach of a gymnast. Evgeni Plushenko (above) performs his *Carmen* program from the Olympic Games. The cast (overleaf) acknowledges the crowd at the end of the opening number.

*I*N TWO HOURS AND 15 MINUTES, the first show was over. Tom Collins had been pleased with many moments, among them the appearance of Michelle Kwan, who received a rousing standing ovation after a perfect performance; then, one skater later, the debut of Sarah Hughes as Olympic gold medalist. She, too, was perfect. She, too, brought down the house. Katarina Witt and Debi Thomas used to do this when they skated together on tour; they invariably rose to the performance level of their rival.

Whether the anything-you-can-do-I-can-do-better performances of Kwan and Hughes were just coincidental or the sign of a friendly little rivalry, no one knew. But one thing was certain: one stellar exhibition performance begat another that night in Florida.

Soon, the buses pulled out of Daytona Beach and headed southwest, to Orlando and another show on another night. As they hit the highway, Tom Collins stood up in front of his bus and called for everyone's attention.

"We had three standing ovations tonight. The finale was wonderful."

He looked up and down the bus, nodding knowingly at all the skaters he had assembled.

"This," he said, "is going to be a great tour."

Gold Miner's Son

*I*T IS FAIR TO SAY THAT TOM COLLINS CAME TO figure skating somewhat reluctantly.

He grew up in a little gold-mining village in northern Ontario called Kirkland Lake, and, like all the other boys in town, while his father worked deep inside the earth, he played on the ice on top of it.

"It was a mining city and a hockey city," he said. "I really wanted to be a hockey player, but I tried it and it didn't work. When I scored a goal on my team, I soon realized that this was not the career for me."

The mines beckoned, but it was the ice that always turned Tom Collins' head. Someone suggested that he try figure skating.

"I had a good stride and I was a fast skater, so I did," he said.

Collins was little more than a teenager, but his way in life soon was set. He would turn his wanderlust for adventure and his affinity for humor into a lifelong endeavor, with a personal history that would end up paralleling the story of American skating shows and tours in the second half of the 20th century.

"I got so into it," he said, "that I would eat, sleep and breathe figure skating. That's all I wanted to do."

The Collins family of Kirkland Lake, Ontario, in 1938: Tom's mother Martha, father James, sister Marty and Tom, then seven years old. James Collins worked in the mines; Martha Collins was a school teacher.

Tom's older sister, Martha (Marty), left Kirkland Lake to travel to the United States to try her luck at a career with a touring hotel show. Wherever she went, from Dallas to Cincinnati to Chicago's Conrad Hilton Hotel, she would send her brother postcards and letters detailing the wonderful life she found for herself on the road, skating.

This was the 1940s, a magical time for figure skating. The great Sonja Henie had arrived in the United States in 1936 after winning her third Olympic gold medal. For more than a decade, she commanded the rapt attention of audiences at ice shows and in movie theaters, becoming, in the words of cigar-chomping sportswriters, "The greatest box office draw in the history of sport."

How could a young man not want to take a flying leap onto this enchanting stage?

For two summers, Collins worked in the mines to pay for his skating lessons. Then, in the summer of 1949, at the age of 18, he received a telegram from Holiday on Ice informing him that he had been accepted as a skater for the show and should report to the Sports Arena in Toledo, Ohio, on August 28, 1949.

He started as a chorus skater, performing in 10 numbers every night, with a salary of $35 a week during rehearsals, then $65 a week when the tour opened. He had to pay for his own food and lodging. Some hotels charged $1.50 a night for a room with no air conditioning.

Obviously, Tom Collins wasn't getting rich on the ice.

In every success story, there's the big break, and Collins' came this way: In his second year with Holiday on Ice, the show's star, Murray Galbraith, became sick. Galbraith was the brother of Sheldon Galbraith,

Young Tom Collins (partially hidden, top row, third from left) joined his father (top row, second from right) in the gold mines for two summers in the 1940s to pay for his skating lessons.

Tom Collins and his first skating partner, Elsie Webster, in 1945 (left). Comedy has always been near and dear to Collins' heart. Below, Collins with partner Paul Andre.

the coach of 1948 Olympic champion Barbara Ann Scott and the man who had given Tom Collins skating lessons back in Schumacker, Ontario. Tom was Murray's understudy, so he took over.

"The number was called Rumble-ero, a Latin-type number," Collins said. "The little kid from Kirkland Lake looked like the village idiot with these frills on my sleeve, a little kerchief around my neck and these white buckskin skates. The first show was outside, in Charlotte, N.C., at some baseball stadium. But I did okay."

For this number, Collins was paid an extra 75 cents a show. "I was a teenager. I thought, 75 cents? That's a lot of money."

Collins soon moved into comedy and pairs skating, then graduated to a solo act, and by the early 1960s, he was the star of Holiday on Ice. His salary was $250 a week, a king's ransom at the time.

These days, top skaters on his tour make 300 times that.

During that second year of the show when Collins stood in for Galbraith, he also arranged to have his sister Marty join Holiday on Ice. His tour was traveling by train, going through Chicago on the way to Salt Lake City. Marty Collins was skating at the Conrad Hilton in Chicago and came to the train station to visit her brother.

"She was a very, very pretty lady, and she got the attention of the producer and director of the show," Tom Collins said. After Tom waved goodbye to his sister and the train pulled out of the station, the director asked Tom if his sister might want to join Holiday on Ice as a chorus skater.

"No problem," Collins said, trying to do anything he could to get ahead. "You've got her."

He called his sister at the next stop to tell her the good news.

"You did what?" Marty Collins screamed into the phone.

"I got you a job with Holiday on Ice," Tom Collins repeated.

"I wouldn't join that rag-tag show if my life depended on it."

"Marty," Tom Collins pleaded, "If you don't join the show, I'm going to get fired."

He didn't get fired. She joined the show.

Two years later, Marty Collins married the show's owner, Morris Chalfen. She eventually quit skating and had three children in the 1950s.

On March 17, 1960, Marty, the three little children and their nanny boarded a flight in Minneapolis to attend the opening of Holiday on Ice in Miami. Tom waited for them at the airport in Miami with his future wife Jane and his brother Butch.

The Kirkland Lake Community Skating Rink was home to Tom Collins (above) when he wasn't in the mines or working odd jobs around town to pay for his skating lessons. As a star in Holiday on Ice (right), Tom Collins was called "smooth as satin."

"The plane kept being delayed and delayed and delayed," Tom said. "Finally, somebody said they heard there was a plane crash. We all hung around the airport until we got the word that a plane had gone down in Tell City, Indiana, and all 63 people aboard were dead."

"*T*HAT," COLLINS SAID, "changed my life."

Knowing he couldn't skate forever, he had recently been seeking advice from his sister.

"Why don't you get into management?" she asked him.

"Maybe I'll do that one day," he replied. "Yeah, maybe one day."

After the plane crash, Collins spoke to the producers of the show. "This is my last year," he said. "I'm going to retire." They laughed at him, so Collins went to Chalfen.

"Your wife — my sister — wanted me to go into management," he said, "so I'm going to do it."

In 1962, Collins left the ice and moved into an office. He became Holiday on Ice's treasurer. "I had never paid a bill in my life," he said. "I made mistakes about 90 percent of the time when I wrote checks."

By the mid-1960s, he was manager of the show, which included a chorus skater named Jane Morris, a former Miss Georgia. Collins began dating Morris, and they were married in 1967. Children soon came along — their three sons: Michael, Mark and Marty.

Collins continued to work his way up the ladder at Holiday on Ice, eventually becoming vice president. But he grew tired of his desk job with the show, and with a young family back home in Minneapolis, he left Holiday on Ice in 1971.

He decided to try something entirely different: he began promoting rock-and-roll singers, including Alice Cooper; Crosby, Stills, Nash and Young; David Bowie; and Earth, Wind and Fire. He had made contacts with the music industry through skating and thought his experience in one field might translate to another.

Marty Collins, Tom's older sister, left home before her brother did to join a touring hotel show in the United States. She performed at the old Stevens Hotel in Chicago with Jerry Mapes (left). Below, Marty and her husband Morris Chalfen in Moscow.

It didn't. By 1974, he was broke. He was forced to cash in his wife's life insurance policy, which gave him about $3,800. He was borrowing money from his parents and his in-laws. He grew concerned that he would lose his house.

One day, Patrick Stansfield, Neil Diamond's production manager and a friend of Collins' from the rock-and-roll world, called. Collins answered the phone while sitting at his sons' miniature table in the attic.

"What are you doing?" Stansfield asked.

"Nothing, actually," Collins said. "I am looking for a job."

Stansfield wondered if Collins would be interested in getting into the merchandising business for touring entertainers. It was something Collins had been thinking of as well.

Soon, Collins was selling programs, T-shirts and posters for Diamond.

The business began to build. Diamond led to John Denver, who led to Bob Dylan, the Moody Blues, Wayne Newton, Rick James and Earth, Wind and Fire, to name a few.

"For the first time in eight years," Collins said, "I could put furniture in my house."

"He was traveling more and more," said youngest son Marty Collins, who was named after his late aunt. "I was in Minneapolis with Mom and my brothers and we wouldn't see him for sometimes one month, sometimes two months."

But when Tom Collins came home, everything changed. "He was the Fourth Kid," Marty Collins said. "'No' wasn't in his vocabulary very often."

Exhibit A: When Collins came home from a trip, he would open his garment bag in the bedroom and allow one of his three sons — Mike, Mark or Marty — to crawl in. Then he would zip up the bag, put it over his shoulder, spin in a circle and throw the bag onto the bed.

"Who knows if you landed on your head, your side, whatever," Marty said, "but you'd bounce around and then you'd bounce off the bed and crash to the floor and be in pain.

He'd unzip the bag and look in. 'Are you okay?' he'd say. And we'd say, 'Do it again!'"

As his merchandising business took off, so too did another foray into the skating world. It had begun inauspiciously several years earlier, in 1969, when Morris Chalfen, who was Collins' boss, got the idea to have a small tour of skating stars hit the road after the world championships at the Broadmoor in Colorado Springs. He and Collins got their inspiration from the International Skating Union, which produced a European tour of about 15 cities after each world championships.

Tom Collins' partner in Holiday on Ice, Jinx Clark, became a lifelong friend.

Why not try the same thing in North America, Collins and Chalfen asked themselves. They received permission from the ISU and the U.S. Figure Skating Association, and off they went, visiting eight cities in Canada and seven in the United States with a cast featuring American stars Janet Lynn, Tim Wood, Jo Jo Starbuck and Ken Shelley and the legendary Protopopovs of the Soviet Union.

From that year onward, every time there was a world championships in North America, a band of skaters set out afterward, barnstorming across the continent. This continued throughout the 1970s and into the 1980s.

"In those early years," Collins said, "we used to come in at seven o'clock with two black fiber cases and the show would start at 7:30. We had Scott Hamilton, Peter Carruthers, people like that. We had a banner to cover the hockey boards and put it up with gray duct tape all the way around. We had a little tape recorder that we'd hook up to the building sound system and we'd be ready to go. Now it takes us six hours to set up and about two and a half hours to take down. It's come a long way. In the early years, nobody knew the difference; we got standing ovations and the audience loved the show."

From one year to the next up to the late 1980s, the tour's popularity built. "By 1988, we put that show on sale and it was like Michael Jackson, people lining up, waiting to buy tickets. We had had an Olympics in North America, in Calgary, that was shown live on U.S. television. We had Katarina Witt and Debi Thomas in the Battle of the Carmens and the Battle of the Brians (Boitano and Orser). It was a big year."

But, as pleased as he was with that tour, Collins said, "I didn't think past 1988. I thought after the Olympic year that Katarina Witt and Brian Boitano would join an ice show, Ice Capades or something. That was normal, and we'd wait for the next Olympics or worlds."

Nonetheless, flushed with success and more than a little curious, Collins phoned Boitano and asked him what he was doing in 1989. Boitano said he was doing nothing. Collins called Witt. She said the same thing.

Jane Morris (left, with Alfredo Mendoza) was a chorus skater in Holiday on Ice. In 1967, she married Tom Collins. Just out of the Army, Elvis Presley (above) visits Holiday on Ice and meets brothers Butch (left) and Tom Collins (right).

Tom Collins skated in the same show as the great Sonja Henie in 1954 at the Roxy Theater in New York and on a tour of South America. He and his wife Jane attended a party at Henie's Beverly Hills home in the 1960s.

He flew to Switzerland to meet with Witt, then went on to Moscow to visit the then-Soviet federation to ask about the availability of their stars. Finally, he flew to San Francisco to see Boitano.

By the time Collins got back to Minneapolis, he had the two Olympic gold medalists from the Calgary Games and all the Soviets he wanted — signed, sealed and delivered.

An every-now-and-then thing was about to become an annual tradition.

THE GREAT AND NOT-SO-GREAT, the famous and infamous (Tonya Harding) — they've all skated under the Champions on Ice banner. Along the way, Tom Collins became one of the best known and most beloved people in figure skating: part king-maker, part philanthropist, part doting grandfather and full-time entrepreneur. For his considerable efforts, Collins, who holds dual U.S. and Canadian citizenship, is the only person named to the World, U.S. and Canadian figure skating halls of fame. Also the USFSA headquarters in Colorado Springs is now called the Tom Collins Building.

"Tom is hard working, inventive, aggressive, funny and delightful," said Dick Button. "He has accomplished an enormous amount in the sport. He's a wonderful diplomat and a great entrepreneur. He's one of the major forces in figure skating over the last half of the century."

"Tommy knows the show-business side of our sport so well," said Peggy Fleming, who skated on the tour in 1991. "Tom Collins has helped ease our sport into the entertainment world, into this wonderful showcase for the skaters. In the 1960s, when the ISU had a tour of Europe after the world championships, we'd be shlepping around, not in the most beautiful of hotels, and during the show, they'd just announce your name and you'd go. Tom has changed all that. He makes it so pleasant. He's a father figure to all these skaters. He knows how to make everyone have fun. That's a talent."

"He's got incredible stamina," said choreographer Sarah Kawahara. "After the show, he'll jump on the bus, then get on the plane, then on the plane we'll have another meeting. It's two o'clock in the morning and he's asking, 'So what do we do in 2004?'

"Then we get to the hotel. It's now 3:00 in the

morning. And Tommy's getting the luggage out of the bus. He's just one of the guys, pulling out all this luggage. He does luggage. Here's the man who owns the company. He's the producer of the show. And he does luggage.

"That's the fun and charming thing about him. He's so big but he's never too big to be an equal and pitch in."

Tom Collins' joie de vivre manifests itself in other ways. Until a few years ago, he would drive to one of Minneapolis' dozens of lakes around midnight every night, strap on his in-line skates and take a five-mile spin on the bike path. One night he tripped on a twig and fell face-first onto the pavement.

From that moment on, Tom Collins took up walking.

"He's a thinker, a late-night thinker," Marty Collins said. "He leaves the house at 11:30 or midnight and comes home around 1:00 A.M. He takes a cigar and he's off on his own. He loves that."

Tom Collins is known for many things in the skating world, not the least of which is an enduring sense of generosity. If he's not pushing cash through a taxicab window to friends on their way to dinner,

he's hosting the most anticipated party of the year at the U.S. national championships or taking over a restaurant at the world championships to throw an impromptu gathering for 100 of his closest friends. He has even been known to give up his hotel suite for friends who've come to the show but, at midnight, find themselves without a room.

"And then he sends up room service," Marty Collins said. "Talk about an open-door policy: 'Here, take my suite.'"

But he has never been happy doing any of this alone. He brought his youngest brother, Harris, on board in 1975 as creative director and choreographer, a job Harris held until the day he died of a heart attack backstage in Chicago on the 1996 tour. Harris was 49. Butch, the middle brother, came on board in 1987 as the tour's director of merchandise.

And when they became old enough, the little boys he once tossed around in the garment bag happily joined the old man in the family business.

Oldest son Michael was the first to come onto the tour, in 1991 at the age of 23. He came on board at

The Collins family: Tom and Jane and (left to right) Mark, Marty and Michael.

the entry-level position all the Collins boys first experienced: as a member of the crew, loading in and loading out the equipment at each tour stop.

Middle son Mark was traveling with a band, so he didn't immediately join the family business, but Marty got his feet wet while still in college, joining the tour in progress during the summer to work on the crew.

Gradually, the father moved each son up the ladder. Michael, who turned 35 in the fall of 2002, is the tour manager, gets involved in many business decisions and is heir apparent to his father. Marty, 31, is the tour coordinator, which means he pulls out a map each year and begins to match cities with dates, followed by hotels, flights, charter buses and the like. Mark, 33, is the tour's merchandising director, taking over from his Uncle Butch, who retired in 2001.

Said Marty: "Mike is trying to fill shoes. I am trying to fill arenas."

But there's no doubt who's still in charge: Dear Old Dad.

"If you look at other 70-year-olds, they are not on the road for 93 shows," Marty Collins said. "He really loves to live."

On the third night of the 2002 tour, in Orlando, Tom Collins watched the show from the stands to gauge fan reaction to the various programs, then made his way to the concourse as the crowd filed out. He was about to embark on one of his favorite pastimes on the road: The Unscientific Audience Survey.

Giddy as a little child, Collins looked around.

"Let's get those people!"

He walked up to a group of five women. He did not identify himself.

"Did you enjoy the show?" he asked.

They perked up and all nodded and said that they did.

"Would you come back next year?" he wondered.

They said they would.

"Who are your favorites?"

The women threw out various names: "Michelle, Sarah, Elvis, Rudy…"

Never bothering to tell them who he was, the owner of the show thanked them and moved on to his next victims.

After about 10 minutes, Collins left the concourse smiling. "Isn't that fun?"

Mark, Tom, Michael and Marty Collins (opposite) in Daytona Beach, Fla., at the start of the 2002 tour. (Above) Tom Collins is inducted into the Canadian Figure Skating Hall of Fame.

Less than 12 hours later, at the tour's resort hotel in Orlando, Collins nonchalantly walked outdoors with his briefcase and cell phone to catch the bus for the ride to that afternoon's show in Tampa. The only problem was, the buses weren't there. They had left without him.

"I saw the back of the second bus as it turned out of the driveway," Collins said. "There was no way for me to catch it."

He stood there for a moment, all by himself, a bit perplexed. Then he started laughing. This was perfect, he said to himself. He, Tom Collins — the tour's founder, owner, executive producer and boss — had been left behind by his own tour buses.

Collins dialed son Michael's cell phone. From the bus, Michael answered and heard his father's voice:

"Know who you forgot?"

Five minutes later, one of the two buses dutifully returned to the hotel to pick up the not-so-insignificant man who had been left behind.

25 Years of Champions

The cast of Champions on Ice pose for an unconventional portrait at the start of the 2002 tour. These patriotic costumes were worn in the show's finale.

*I*T BEGAN AS A SMALL SKATING TOUR WITH NO expectations. Owner Tom Collins believed there would never be another one. Just one year and out. That's what he thought.

That, of course, was 34 years and 24 tours ago.

"There was no way to know back then how big skating and the tour would become," Collins said. "We did 15 shows and then everyone went home. I never thought we'd do it again."

He did — three years later. And again, three years after that, and then three years after that. Pretty soon, the Champions on Ice tour was an annual event playing to sold-out arenas with some of the most popular names in all of sports: Peggy Fleming, Dorothy Hamill, Brian Boitano, Katarina Witt, Michelle Kwan.

"Tom Collins proved that there was a market, there was a hunger, to see the best skaters in the world not just on television, but in person, in your city," said Scott Hamilton, who spent three years on the tour in the early 1980s. "The fans watched the Olympics on TV, live, in the United States in 1980, then wanted to see those skaters when they went on tour. It happened again after the 1984 Olympics. This was not an overnight sensation. It developed over time."

And time began in 1969.

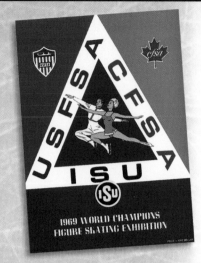

1969 WORLD CHAMPIONS
FIGURE SKATING EXHIBITION

CAST OF SKATERS

Linda Bernard &
Raymond Wilson, GREAT BRITAIN

Linda Carbonetto, CANADA

Patricia Dodd, GREAT BRITAIN

Anna Forder &
Richard Stephens, CANADA

Gundrun Hauss &
Walter Hafner, WEST GERMANY

Julie Holmes, USA

Jay Humphry, CANADA

Ron Kauffman &
Cynthia Kauffman, USA

Janet Lynn, USA

Karen Magnussen, CANADA

Hana Maskova, CZECHOSLOVAKIA

Melissa Militano &
Mark Militano, USA

Ondrej Nepela, CZECHOSLOVAKIA

Patrick Pera, FRANCE

John Misha Petkevich, USA

Ludmila Protopopov &
Oleg Protopopov, USSR

Irina Rodnina &
Alexsei Ulanov, USSR

Janet Schwartz, AUSTRIA

Judy Schwomeyer &
James Sladky, USA

Gabriele Seyfert, EAST GERMANY

Jo Jo Starbuck &
Kenneth Shelley, USA

Heidemarie Steiner &
Heinz Walther, EAST GERMANY

Donna Taylor &
Bruce Lennie, CANADA

Diane Towler &
Bernard Ford, GREAT BRITAIN

Gary Visconti, USA

Tim Wood, USA

Kazumi Yamashita, JAPAN

15 SHOWS

ONLY A PROGRAM remains to tell the story of the beginnings of Champions on Ice. The names are part of figure skating's history: Janet Lynn, Karen Magnussen, Jo Jo Starbuck and Ken Shelley, Irina Rodnina and Alexsei Ulanov, John Misha Petkevich, Ondrej Nepela, Tim Wood.

It all started simply enough. Intrigued by the International Skating Union's tours of Europe after world championships held on the continent, Tom Collins and Morris Chalfen decided to try their hand at organizing a tour after a world championships in the United States. They received the blessing of the U.S. Figure Skating Association after the 1969 worlds in Colorado Springs.

Collins, then vice president and general manager of Holiday on Ice, booked and arranged the tour but did not travel with it. This first year and 1972 were the only times Collins did not travel with the tour.

The skaters went to 15 cities: eight in Canada and seven in the United States. Collins and Chalfen lost about $25,000–30,000 for their efforts.

"We'll never do that again," Collins said at the time.

Years later, he laughs.

"Who thought this thing was going to last?"

Jo Jo Starbuck and Kenneth Shelley were three-time U.S. champions and two-time world bronze medalists in the early 1970s.

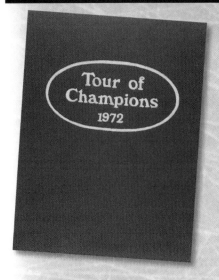

Tour of
Champions
1972

*T*HE 1972 TOUR was hosted by Ice Capades after the Olympic Games in Sapporo, Japan, and brought back many of the stars from 1969, led by Olympic bronze medalist Janet Lynn. Gold medalist Trixi Schuba also was a member of the tour. Canada's Toller Cranston joined for the first time.

Although he was not involved with it, Tom Collins counts this tour, which came after the worlds in Calgary, as part of the lineage of Champions on Ice.

The tour was arranged by George Eby, Ice Capades' president, and Dick Palmer, its vice president.

Olympic bronze medalist Janet Lynn
is considered by many to be the most
beautiful skater in U.S. history.

CAST OF SKATERS

Zsuzsi Almassy, HUNGARY

Angelika Buck &
Erick Buck, WEST GERMANY

Sergei Chetverukin, USSR

Toller Cranston, CANADA

Manuela Gross &
Uwe Kagelmann, EAST GERMANY

Almut Lehman &
Herbert Wiesinger, WEST GERMANY

Janet Lynn, USA

Karen Magnussen, CANADA

Sonja Morgenstern, EAST GERMANY

Ondrej Nepala, CZECHOSLOVAKIA

Ludmila Pakhomova &
Aleksandr Gorshkov, USSR

John Misha Petkevich, USA

Irina Rodnina &
Alexsei Ulanov, USSR

Trixi Schuba, AUSTRIA

Judy Schwomeyer &
James Sladky, USA

Jo Jo Starbuck &
Kenneth Shelley, USA

1975

WORLD FIGURE SKATING TOUR

THE WORLD CHAMPIONSHIPS were back in Colorado Springs, so Tom Collins was back in the skating tour business. "This was the first time I really got heavily involved in this. I was actually at the world championships for the first time."

There, he saw two of the sport's greatest names — John Curry and Dorothy Hamill — win the gold and silver medals, respectively, in the men's and women's competition, and Irina Rodnina, the most decorated pairs skater in history, win her seventh consecutive world title. (There would be three more before her career ended.)

But Collins wasn't the only one watching it all. Back in 10th place in the pairs competition were two American teenagers, Tai Babilonia and Randy Gardner. They performed with the tour during a few stops in California that year.

"We were very young and we got to be around a lot of great skaters we were in awe of, including the Russians and the East Germans," Gardner said.

Within a few years, Rodnina and her second partner, Alexandr Zaitsev, would be their rivals, but, said Gardner in 1975, "we weren't there yet."

Said Babilonia: "I held Irina in such a different place. It didn't even feel like we were competing against her."

"For us at that time, being on the tour was a learning experience, just watching them train and skate," Gardner said.

"It was the best way to tour," added Babilonia. "It was like Alice in Wonderland. For so long, we were always the youngest. There were all these great skaters: Melissa Militano and Johnny Johns, Dorothy Hamill….I was like the baby. You can't believe you're touring and traveling with them. We were the puppies. It was a different world. I don't even know how much we got paid. We got different things free from different companies. Tommy would give us tennis shoes or running shoes and we were elated to get that. It was a very different time."

Said Hamill, who was about to become Olympic champion: "We were just having fun. There was no tension and no stress."

The tour was bare-bones, with nothing more than a banner and a tape recorder to play music over the arena's public address system. At one tour stop, in Quebec City, Collins said there were more people skating on the ice than watching in the stands.

"It was 'Spanky and Our Gang Presents…' Hamill said. "We would truck in with our little costumes and our little skates and we would skate our little programs."

CAST OF SKATERS

Toller Cranston, CANADA

John Curry, GREAT BRITAIN

Dianne de Leeuw, NETHERLANDS

Christine Errath, EAST GERMANY

Manuela Gross &
Uwe Kagelmann, EAST GERMANY

Dorothy Hamill, USA

Romy Kermer &
Rolf Oesterreich, EAST GERMANY

Vladimir Kovalev, USSR

Terry Kubicka, USA

Gordon McKellen, Jr., USA

Melissa Militano &
Johnny Johns, USA

Irina Moiseeva &
Andrei Minenkov, USSR

Lynn Nightingale, CANADA

Colleen O'Connor &
Jim Millns, USA

Ludmila Pakhomova &
Aleksandr Gorshkov, USSR

Irina Rodnina &
Alexandr Zaitsev, USSR

Sergei Volkov, USSR

WORLD 1975 FIGURE SKATING TOUR EXHIBITION BY THE '75 WORLD CHAMPIONS

John Curry, the 1976
Olympic gold medalist, later
went on to form his own
renowned touring company.

Soviet pair Irina
Rodnina and Alexandr
Zaitsev won Olympic
gold medals in 1976
and 1980.

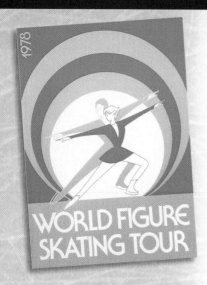

WORLD FIGURE SKATING TOUR

CAST OF SKATERS

Lisa-Marie Allen, USA

Tai Babilonia &
Randy Gardner, USA

Robin Cousins, GREAT BRITAIN

Susanna Driano, ITALY

Linda Fratianne, USA

Jan Hoffmann, EAST GERMANY

Fumio Igarashi, JAPAN

Natalia Linichuk &
Gennadi Karponosov, USSR

Manuela Mager &
Uwe Bewersdorff, EAST GERMANY

Anett Poetzsch, EAST GERMANY

Krisztina Regoeczy &
Andras Sallay, HUNGARY

Irina Rodnina &
Alexandr Zaitsev, USSR

Stacey Smith &
John Summers, USA

Janet Thompson &
Warren Maxwell, GREAT BRITAIN

Charles Tickner, USA

Lorna Wighton &
John Dowding, CANADA

$\mathcal{A}$FTER THE WORLD championships in Ottawa, Tom Collins brought together a group of skaters heading straight for the 1980 Olympic Games in Lake Placid, N.Y. Included were American Linda Fratianne, who would win a controversial silver medal at the Olympics, East Germany's Anett Poetzsch, the gold medalist, and England's Robin Cousins and East Germany's Jan Hoffman, the future gold and silver medalists, respectively, in the Olympic men's competition.

It wasn't only the skaters who came along for the ride. Parents and coaches and federation officials all had a seat on the bus.

"The rule with the ISU was whatever coaches wanted to go, we had to take them," Collins said. "If parents wanted to come along, we had to take them too."

When the show reached Oakland, Collins began a tradition of inviting up-and-coming skaters to perform in front of the local audience. He asked a gangly 14-year-old, the new junior men's national champion, to join the show for the evening.

Little did Collins know that this nervous young man would end up as the cornerstone of his tour, performing in 12 summer tours and six winter tours of Champions on Ice.

It was Brian Boitano.

Linda Fratianne followed Dorothy Hamill as the brightest skating star in the United States, winning the world championships in 1977 and 1979 before settling for a controversial silver medal at the 1980 Olympics.

England's Robin Cousins (left) won the Olympic gold medal in 1980 but never won a world title. (Below) The group photo became a tour tradition. Tom Collins is kneeling in front of the skaters; young Tai Babilonia and Randy Gardner are in the back row, third and fourth from the left.

1 On the bus, 1997: Brian Boitano,
Michelle Kwan and Tara Lipinski;
2 Tim Goebel;
3 Paul Wylie, 1992;
4 Elvis Stojko;
5 Back on the bus;
6 Nicole Bobek and Rudy Galindo;
7 Stopping for milkshakes;
8 Unloading at the latest stop on tour.

On The Road Again

CHRISTOPHER BOWMAN spent the night in it. Elvis Stojko was left behind by it. There have been wedding showers held on it. And the number of cell phone calls coming from it can exceed those of some small countries.

It's the Champions on Ice tour bus.

"The bus is about 90 percent of your experience on the tour," said Randy Gardner. "You spend so much darn time on it."

"The best stuff happens on the bus rides," Tai Babilonia said.

"It's where you really get to know people," Gardner added. "Or you have your own space. You read or sleep or do whatever you need to do before you get to the next city."

"That's what it's all about on the bus, sleeping," said Brian Boitano. "And the late-night truck stops. Tommy Collins is notorious for his stops. We'll pull into this small town and a busload of skaters will get off at 2:00 in the morning at a truck stop. Or we'll stop at a 7-Eleven. People will just pile up on junk food at the 7-Eleven. Tom pays for everybody's snacks at 2:00 in the morning."

To sleep or not to sleep, that is the question.

"It always takes us a couple of hours for everyone to wind down," Babilonia said. "Rudy Galindo in particular is extremely wound up after a show. One day, I was just so tired and just didn't feel like joking or laughing, and Rudy can go on non-stop. So I said, 'Rudy, can you just shut up for five minutes? Just try it.'

"Well, everyone got really quiet, and he shut his mouth, but the thing is, he shut his mouth for the rest of the bus ride because he was so angry at me, and the rest of the day and even into the next day. He didn't say a word to me. Then I felt really bad. I tried to talk to him, and he wouldn't look at me. He even

zipped his lips shut. I felt horrible."

Some bus moments have become the stuff of legend. Bowman had been out so late one night that he was afraid he would oversleep and miss the bus. So he solved that problem by opening the door to the bay of the bus — the luggage hold — and crawling in. When the driver started loading bags that morning, he discovered Bowman, sound asleep.

In St. Louis one year, Stojko hopped onto the bus, put down his bag, and, with five minutes to spare before the departure time, decided to run and grab a McDonald's. He saw Jerod Swallow as he left the bus. "Please make sure they don't leave without me," Stojko said.

When he returned with his hamburger, the bus was gone, on its way to Peoria, Ill.

These were the days before cell phones were in vogue, so Stojko had to improvise. He raced to the airport, booked a flight to Peoria, and arrived 15 minutes before the show began.

Stojko's first words as he arrived at the arena?

"Where's Jerod?"

There actually are two buses, known affectionately as the "American bus" and the "Russian bus." Anyone can get on either bus. Americans ride with the international skaters, and vice versa. And on special occasions, there is a "boys' bus" and a "girls' bus," such as the time the women all dressed in their PJ's for a combination slumber party/wedding shower for Jenni Meno.

Usually, it's all a blur. "You're on the bus, on your cell phone, talking to someone," said performance director Brian Klavano, "and they ask, 'Where are you?' And you say, 'I don't know.' We cross so many state lines, if we were changing currency, we'd be in trouble."

1980

1980 OLYMPIC FIGURE SKATING TOUR

CAST OF SKATERS

Lisa-Marie Allen, USA

Judy Blumberg &
Michael Seibert, USA

Kitty Carruthers &
Peter Carruthers, USA

Carol Fox &
Richard Dalley, USA

Sheryl Franks &
Michael Botticelli, USA

Scott Hamilton, USA

Fumio Igarashi, JAPAN

Sandy Lenz, USA

Brian Pockar, CANADA

Liliana Rehakova &
Stanislav Drastich, CZECHOSLOVAKIA

David Santee, USA

Stacey Smith &
John Summers, USA

Charles Tickner, USA

Kristina Wegelius, FINLAND

Lorna Wighton &
John Dowding, CANADA

Elaine Zayak, USA

12 SHOWS

FOR THE FIRST TIME ever, Tom Collins hosted a tour after the Olympic Games, an Olympics held in Lake Placid, N.Y. He called it the 1980 Olympic Figure Skating Tour, as the banner proudly proclaims at the Broadmoor World Arena in Colorado Springs. This was one of five names that the tour has been known by since its inception.

It was also Collins' first encounter with Scott Hamilton, who had finished fifth in the 1980 Olympics. "He was very entertaining," Collins said. "He did his chicken number. It brought the house down."

Other American newcomers who caught Collins' eye were Elaine Zayak and the brother-and-sister pairs team of Kitty and Peter Carruthers.

"I had a lot of Americans," Collins said. "It wasn't that international, not that year. I was getting a warmer feeling for the skaters. I started wondering if maybe there was some kind of a thing we could do here on an annual basis.

"The buildings started asking, 'Why don't you do it every year?'

"I said, 'Are you kidding? I'm having a hard enough time doing it every three years.'"

Trying to come up with innovative ways to sell his show, Collins thought about signing speed skater Eric Heiden, the winner of five Olympic gold medals, to participate in some way.

"I thought it would add something," Collins said. "But I couldn't figure out how to incorporate speed skating into a figure skating show, so it never went anywhere."

Four-time U.S. champion Charles Tickner (opposite) had a banner season in 1980: a U.S. national title and Olympic and world bronze medals. Elaine Zayak (right) stunned the skating world, and herself, by winning the world championships in 1982 with a flurry of triple jumps. She finished sixth at the 1984 Olympic Games.

1980 OLYMPIC FIGURE SKATING TOUR

A presentation by the exciting performers from the National, World and Olympic Figure Skating Championships

SUNDAY, APRIL 27
8 PM • MET CENTER
BLOOMINGTON

15 SHOWS

$\mathcal{A}$NOTHER WORLD CHAMPIONSHIPS in the United States, this one in Hartford, another skating tour that followed. This was one of the two Champions on Ice appearances of the great Jayne Torvill and Christopher Dean, still three years away from their Olympic gold-medal-winning performance in Sarajevo.

They won the first of four consecutive world titles that year, then crossed the United States for the first time ever.

"It was a big deal to do that tour across America," Dean said. "It was an exciting thing. We had never roomed with other skaters or been around many American skaters. It also opened our eyes to what the audience was thinking. We had been so channeled to what the judges were thinking. Being on the tour made us broader minded. I think it made us better skaters and performers."

CAST OF SKATERS

Lisa-Marie Allen, USA

Sabine Baess &
Tassilo Thierbach, EAST GERMANY

Natalia Bestemianova &
Andrei Bukin, USSR

Denise Biellmann, SWITZERLAND

Judy Blumberg &
Michael Seibert, USA

Igor Bobrin, USSR

Kitty Carruthers &
Peter Carruthers, USA

Deborah Cottrill, GREAT BRITAIN

Scott Hamilton, USA

Fumio Igarashi, Japan

Marie McNeil &
Rob McCall, CANADA

Irina Moiseeva &
Andrei Minenkov, USSR

Brian Orser, CANADA

David Santee, USA

Jayne Torvill &
Christopher Dean, GREAT BRITAIN

Barbara Underhill &
Paul Martini, CANADA

Irina Vorobieva &
Igor Lisovsky, USSR

Robert Wagenhoffer, USA

Tracey Wainman, CANADA

Katarina Witt, EAST GERMANY

Elaine Zayak, USA

Denise Biellmann of Switzerland won the world title in 1981 but will always be better known for the spin that bears her name.

Scott Hamilton honed his
performing skills by skating
with the tour for three
seasons before winning the
Olympic gold medal in 1984.

England's Jayne Torvill and
Christopher Dean considered their
first tour across America in 1981 to
be an important step in their journey
to the top of their sport.

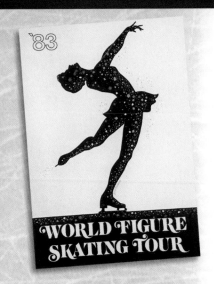

'83

WORLD FIGURE SKATING TOUR

CAST OF SKATERS

Karen Barber &
Nicky Slater, GREAT BRITAIN

Judy Blumberg &
Michael Seibert, USA

Kitty Carruthers &
Peter Carruthers, USA

Mark Cockerell, USA

Vikki DeVries, USA

Carol Fox &
Richard Dalley, USA

Scott Hamilton, USA

Lea Ann Miller &
William Fauver, USA

Brian Orser, CANADA

Veronika Pershina &
Marat Akbarov, USSR

Norbert Schramm, WEST GERMANY

Elisa Spitz &
Scott Gregory, USA

Rosalynn Sumners, USA

Kay Thomson, CANADA

Barbara Underhill &
Paul Martini, CANADA

Olga Volozhinskaya &
Alexandre Svinin, USSR

Jill Watson &
Burt Lancon, USA

Tracy Wilson &
Rob McCall, CANADA

17 SHOWS

TOM COLLINS DID something different in 1983. The world championships were not in North America but in Helsinki, Finland. Nonetheless, Collins decided to host another tour, this one all in the United States.

Collins didn't have Seattle on the schedule of 16 shows, but when Rosalynn Sumners, who grew up in Seattle, won the world championship, he tacked her hometown onto the end of the tour.

The tour also played Boston Garden for the first time. It was a stop that Canadian ice dancer Tracy Wilson remembers well.

"I was a starving artist, a starving student, a starving athlete," she said. "I had moved to Toronto and rented a basement apartment and bought my appliances at Goodwill and was just trying to make ends meet. Tommy asked us [Tracy and her partner, the late Rob McCall] to go on the tour. We had won the Canadian championship in 1982 and 1983, and this was our introduction to the big time.

"I remember being on the ice at Boston Garden, and at that time, for the opening number, you'd crouch in the darkness beside the boards until it was your turn to be introduced. And I remember hearing the audience, the cheering from the audience as I was crouching down, and my knees started shaking. I didn't know how I was going to get to center ice with Rob. We made it, but it was a moment I'll never forget, coming from a small town, living in a basement apartment, and now there I was in Boston Garden."

Ice dancers Judy Blumberg and Michael Seibert (top) won three consecutive world bronze medals and five U.S. titles in the 1980s. Brother and sister pair Peter and Kitty Carruthers (above) would go on to win the 1984 Olympic silver medal in Sarajevo. Rosalynn Sumners (right) won the world championships in 1983 but lost the Olympic gold medal the next year to Katarina Witt by the narrowest of margins.

WORLD FIGURE SKATING TOUR 1983

Gotta Laugh

*I*T WAS NO SURPRISE to Dan Hollander that he was dressed as a woman night after night on the 2002 tour of Champions on Ice.

"The very first time I actually saw a skating show, I was seven years old at Joe Louis Arena in Detroit, and this guy comes out in a chicken outfit," Hollander said.

"It was Scott Hamilton. I was crying, I was laughing so hard. And I thought how cool it would be if I could ever do this, if I could ever make people laugh."

That was 1980.

"I kind of forgot about it. And then, in 1996, when Tommy [Collins] invited me on the tour, I'm doing a janitor routine, and during the intermission, I'm in the tunnel that goes to the ice, and this little teeny girl learned over and said, 'Look, Mommy, there's the funny guy.'

"All of a sudden, it hit home: being that young once myself, seeing a show for the first time, laughing at the guy in the chicken outfit, and now there was a girl giggling at me. I had come full circle."

If Tom Collins doesn't hear the audience laughing during his show, he doesn't believe it has been a successful evening.

"People accuse me of going back and delving into my ice show past because we used to have this type of comedy," Collins said, "and they're absolutely right. Look back just a few years ago; we never had Dan Hollander's style of comedy, or the Ukranian acrobats, or any of this in the show.

"This was an exhibition of the world and Olympic

champions," he said, "and that's all there was, figure skating for two-plus hours. If you're not a connoisseur or an ice skating buff, it does get boring after a while. I'm on the prowl all the time to get novelty in the show, classy novelty."

In 2002, Ukranian acrobats Oleksiy Polishchuk and Vladimir Besedin dressed in white tutus and performed as a most unlikely pair of ballerinas to "Swan Lake." Collins also asked Rudy Galindo to bring back his crowd-pleasing "Y-M-C-A" program and encouraged Isabelle Brasseur and Lloyd Eisler to perform for the third time in their 13 years on tour in drag, she as a man and he as a woman in a program called "She Ain't Pretty."

He positioned Galindo and Brasseur and Eisler as the last two numbers of the first act of the show. This wasn't a coincidence. "I love the way the first act ends," Collins said.

"This is the third time we've done this, each one different with different music," Eisler said of their gender reversal. "We did it in 1991, then we did it again in 1996. Tommy's always been wanting us to do it again, and we've always said 'No, we want to come up with new ideas.' But [2002] technically was our last summer tour, and we always said in our last year, we'd do it again, so he wanted it and we wanted to do it."

Sometimes laughter comes when you least expect it. In the early 1990s, Viktor Petrenko remembers playing Atlanta with his number "Twist Again." He always invited a woman or girl in the front row to dance with him as the number began. Always, the spectator stayed in her row. But this time, Petrenko was very surprised to see the woman he chose jump over the boards and join him on the ice.

"I danced with her for 10 seconds," he said, "and then I thought I should go and do my number. Well, she tried to get back to her seat, but the boards, they were quite high, and she couldn't get back over. As I performed my number, one of my eyes was watching what she was doing. I realized the audience was not watching me, they were watching her. When she got close to making it over, the crowd went, 'Ahhhhh.'

"By the end of my number, she finally made it. She got great applause — more than I did, as a matter of fact."

Audience participation is the essence of Philippe Candeloro's act. That, and taking off his clothes.

"Sometimes I play too much to the audience," Candeloro said. "But I am French, I'm Philippe. You can't change me from Philippe to become Todd Eldredge."

There's a strategy to picking out women to kiss in the audience, Candeloro said.

"I never choose the girls before the show starts. I see people as I skate by, I look for people who are very excited. If I go there, it's going to be more exciting for everybody. It's better to pick somebody who has good company around them. So, of course, it's better to go to someone who is very excited, but two seats away, there might be a shy woman, and I like to pick the shy woman sometimes too. It may be the first time for her to have a chance to pass over her shyness, so I pick her.

"And sometimes," Candeloro continued, "they are saying, 'I hope it's not going to be me, I hope it's not going to be me,' and I pick one of those women sometimes. I change my mind sometimes too. Some grab me and won't let me go. I say, 'I have to go, I have to go,' and everyone is laughing, but she's very happy and she doesn't want to let me go. The people in America, they are very nice, because they like to play."

For Collins, that's the magic of a skating show. "Laughter is wonderful," he said. "Laughter is everything."

He has assembled some true believers on his tour.

"If you fall when you're doing comedy, you make it part of your act," Hollander said. "Every night, I try to incorporate something different, maybe do a break-dancing granny one night, or something like that, so I keep myself amused."

Hollander says "a life sitting at home watching cartoons" led him to his role as the class clown of the tour.

"The applause is great," he said, "but in the middle of a routine, if I hear a little kid giggling hysterically at me, that's what makes it for me."

'84 TOUR OF OLYMPIC & WORLD FIGURE SKATING CHAMPIONS

CAST OF SKATERS

Sabine Baess &
Tassilo Thierbach, EAST GERMANY

Karen Barber &
Nicky Slater, GREAT BRITAIN

Natalia Bestemianova &
Andrei Bukin, USSR

Kitty Carruthers &
Peter Carruthers, USA

Rudi Cerne, WEST GERMANY

Alexandr Fadeev, USSR

Scott Hamilton, USA

Marina Klimova &
Sergei Ponomarenko, USSR

Anna Kondrasheva, USSR

Brian Orser, CANADA

Rosalynn Sumners, USA

Kay Thomson, CANADA

Barbara Underhill &
Paul Martini, CANADA

Elena Valova &
Oleg Vasiliev, USSR

Tracy Wilson &
Rob McCall, CANADA

Katarina Witt, EAST GERMANY

Elaine Zayak, USA

THE SKATING TOUR BUSINESS picked up considerably in an Olympic year, Tom Collins was learning.

Collins had scheduled seven Canadian cities and eight U.S. cities but then added seven more U.S. dates once the tour was underway. Why? For the first time ever, spectators were fascinated by the tour. Average attendance was 10,000 per show.

In 1984, there had been the Games in Sarajevo, then the world championships in Ottawa. In the pairs competition, Soviets Elena Valova and Oleg Vasiliev won the gold at the Olympics, while Canadians Barbara Underhill and Paul Martini won the world title in their homeland.

"I don't remember any whistles or shouts of 'Russian go home' as we were on the tour," said Tamara Moskvina, the coach of the Soviet pair. "The response of the public was very good, even back then. Skating in America, they had to have their heroes from America, but we were treated quite well. Everything was taken care of. The buses were good. The food was good. Tom Collins was spending money to make the life of the skaters very good. He was making the skaters happy."

"A lot of people forget that the ISU still mandated what we received as an honorarium," Martini said. "It was like $200 a show. That's what we got paid. So Tommy used to flip us extra cash by putting bunting on the boards and hauling bags off the luggage carousel. Those days, it was simply skaters and a bus, so the extra work and extra money worked well for everyone.

"At that time, Tommy's tour was the only opportunity, it was the one and only," Martini continued. "This brought to the forefront that people weren't coming to see you compete. They came to see you perform. We were on a pretty steep learning curve because we had little experience performing. We hadn't had the opportunity to explore that side of skating because we were too busy jumping through hoops. It was our first taste of everything: traveling, skating with everybody from the upper echelon of the sport. All of us had done little club shows, but this was very different. It provided us with a huge source of motivation as we moved along with our careers."

This was Brian Boitano's first real taste of tour life as well.

"I saw the crowd going wild with the stars of the 1984 Olympics," he said, "and I thought, man, that's what I really want."

Katarina Witt won the first of her two Olympic gold medals in 1984 in Sarajevo.

Tour alums Torvill and Dean (above) won the Olympic gold medal with a string of perfect 6.0s for *Bolero* at the Sarajevo Olympics. Scott Hamilton (right) was a crowd favorite at the 1984 Games — and that hasn't changed in the two decades that have followed.

15 SHOWS

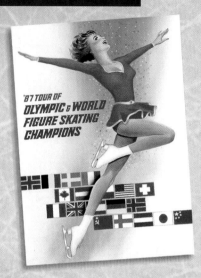

'87 TOUR OF **OLYMPIC & WORLD FIGURE SKATING CHAMPIONS**

CAST OF SKATERS

1 Natalia Bestemianova &
2 Andrei Bukin, USSR
3 Brian Boitano, USA
4 Christopher Bowman, USA
5 Cynthia Coull &
6 Mark Rowson, CANADA
7 Alexandr Fadeev, USSR
8 Ekaterina Gordeeva &
9 Sergei Grinkov, USSR
10 Caryn Kadavy, USA
11 Marina Klimova &
12 Sergei Ponomarenko, USSR
13 Vladimir Kotin, USSR
   Elizabeth Manley, CANADA
14 Brian Orser, CANADA
15 Suzanne Semanick &
   Scott Gregory, USA

16 Debi Thomas, USA
17 Jill Trenary, USA
   Elena Valova &
   Oleg Vasiliev, USSR
18 Jill Watson &
19 Peter Oppegard, USA
20 Tracy Wilson &
21 Rob McCall, CANADA
22 Katarina Witt, EAST GERMANY

ALSO...

A Tom Collins
B Harris Collins
C Elaine DeMore
D Natalia Dubova
E Marilyn Lowey
F Bob Mach
G Jutta Mueller
H Tatiana Tarasova

LONG AGO, THE FACES stopped being new to us.

These are some of the most recognizable names in figure skating: Ekaterina Gordeeva and Sergei Grinkov, Katarina Witt, Debi Thomas, Brian Boitano, Brian Orser.

But they had to start their performing careers somewhere.

"Gordeeva and Grinkov," Tom Collins said their names slowly. "What stood out the most was he was so big and she was so small. She was like a little doll, a little rag doll, she was so thin and small. He just tossed her around in the air. It was unbelievable."

The world championships in Cincinnati provided a strong boost for Collins' tour. The women's competition there had been superb. Debi Thomas, suffering from Achilles tendinitis in both feet, applied ice shavings from an ice-making machine to her ankles before she skated. She performed magnificently, landing all five of her triple jumps. "Debi skated perfectly," Collins said. "Everyone's thinking, Witt's dead."

With the audience still roaring, Witt coolly stepped onto the ice. Thomas came out to watch. Amazingly, Witt tried five triple jumps, even though no one thought she could *do* five triple jumps. On one, the landing was slightly flawed. Otherwise, she, too, was perfect. Witt received a 6.0 from the East German judge — now there was a surprise — and won the world title, with Thomas finishing second.

"It was like 1996 when Michelle Kwan defeated Lu Chen at the worlds in Edmonton," Collins said.

When she came onto his tour, Witt showed up with a hat for her number. "It was something about Jutta Mueller [Witt's coach] and the East Germans," Collins said. "Witt always wore a hat for exhibitions."

But this was Katarina Witt. Collins would take her any way he could get her.

Debi Thomas won a world title in 1986 and was on her way to a classic showdown with Katarina Witt at the 1988 Calgary Olympics.

Jill Watson and Peter Oppegard (right) won three U.S. titles and the 1988 Olympic bronze medal. The gold medalists that year were Ekaterina Gordeeva and Sergei Grinkov of the Soviet Union (below).

Mark Collins and Eric Lang

Marty Collins and Paul Hendrickson

Move 'em In, Move 'em Out

PAUL HENDRICKSON stood in the arena loading dock late at night in the midst of a four-and-a-half month, coast-to-coast odyssey. Sweaty workers were pushing heavy cases around him, guiding them from the arena toward five semis parked outside. As he oversaw the operation, he occasionally joined in and helped the stage hands by nudging along a particularly heavy crate. Then, when the last of the trucks was packed and it came time to sleep, he and his crew curled up in bunks on a moving bus and woke up in the morning inside a different arena, in a different city, in a different state.

"People always say, 'Geez, you're in the entertainment business. Isn't it glamorous?'" said Hendrickson, the tour production manager. "People show up for a concert and say, 'Isn't that nice?' They have no idea how it got here."

Nor do they know how it leaves. Within five minutes after the last skater steps off the ice in the finale each night, the tunnel he or she walked through is gone. Packed up. Heading to the truck.

Within 15 minutes, a spectator returning to the seats for an item left behind wouldn't recognize the place. A score of cases litters the ice, and a dozen thick wires are hanging from the ceiling, giving the appearance of streaking rain. These wires are bringing tons of sound and lighting equipment slowly back to earth, with the help of six workers in the rafters. Once, on a different show, a worker fell out of a lighting truss and landed feet first into a piano on stage.

"He lived to tell about it," Hendrickson said.

There are no mishaps on this night. Within two-and-a-half hours, 273,500 pounds of equipment has been safely packed into the trucks by 16 traveling crew members and 40 to 45 local stage hands.

Only the ice remains behind.

They hit the highway together, the five trucks and the crew bus, and it's often a serious road trip. After packing up a matinee in Fort Lauderdale one day, the crew drove 639 miles to Atlanta for a show the next evening. One of the trucks carries 80,000 souvenir programs in boxes, to be sold at concession stands night after night.

Another carries the fireworks used by the 2002 tour in the finale. "We put them in the back," says driver Jim Means, "as far as possible away from me."

The skaters come to know and appreciate what the crew does. On more than one occasion in the 1990s, Nancy Kerrigan and Isabelle Brasseur pushed cases backstage and helped to put together the rigging for the sound and lighting system.

Each of the three Collins brothers began his tour career on Hendrickson's crew. When Michael joined the crew in the early 1990s, one of his duties was setting up his father's office each night. When the tour rolled into Boston Garden, Michael went about putting together the office — until he realized he was missing his father's six-by-eight-foot rug. Michael found Hendrickson to tell him the rug must have been left behind in Hartford. He wanted to know what he should do.

"I told him he better get it," Hendrickson said.

So Michael took a cab to Boston's Logan Airport, rented a small car, drove to Hartford and found the rug. To make room for it in his rental car, he opened the passenger side window and drove back to Boston with the rug sticking out of the car. Unfortunately for Collins, it started raining…hard.

"When I got back to Boston, the rug was soaked," Collins said. "I gained a great appreciation for the crew that day."

CAST OF SKATERS

1 Natalia Bestemianova &
2 Andrei Bukin, USSR

3 Brian Boitano, USA

4 Christopher Bowman, USA
  Kurt Browning, CANADA

  Isabelle Duchesnay &
  Paul Duchesnay, FRANCE

5 Alexandr Fadeev, USSR

  Karyn Garossino &
  Rod Garossino, CANADA

6 Christine Hough &
7 Doug Ladret, CANADA

8 Caryn Kadavy, USA

9 Marina Klimova &
10 Sergei Ponomarenko, USSR

11 Vladimir Kotin, USSR

12 Elizabeth Manley, CANADA

13 Brian Orser, CANADA

14 Viktor Petrenko, USSR

Natalie Seybold &
Wayne Seybold, USA

15 Debi Thomas, USA

16 Jill Trenary, USA

17 Elana Valova &
18 Oleg Vasiliev, USSR

Gillian Wachsman &
Todd Waggoner, USA

19 Jill Watson &
20 Peter Oppegard, USA

21 Tracy Wilson &
22 Rob McCall, CANADA

23 Katarina Witt, EAST GERMANY

24 Paul Wylie, USA

Susan Wynne &
Joseph Druar, USA

ALSO...

A Tom Collins
B Harris Collins
C Rudy Blinov
D Bob Mach

"THE 1988 TOUR was just magical," said Jill Trenary, the fourth-place finisher at the 1988 Olympics in Calgary, "because of the closeness of the group we had. It all seemed so new and exciting. There was Brian, Katarina, Debi. There was such energy coming from the audience, and we appreciated it. We all felt so fortunate to be on the tour. It really was magical."

"That's when we started doing 15,000 people a night," Tom Collins said. "The Battle of the Brians, the Battle of the Carmens, prime time, ABC, Calgary. The day we opened up ticket sales, people were lined up around the block. We started in Cincinnati and finished in Cincinnati. We added a date there. We started with 24 dates and we added 10 more, all in the United States."

Said Collins: "It was magic to me. We started the overture and people in the building would just cheer. People had not seen these skaters before in person. They had seen them on TV. The excitement in the building was incredible. And everybody who skated got these tremendous ovations. Not like now, because people are so used to it now. This was the beginning, the infancy of the standing ovations and the fans going on forever. And everybody would do encores. Brian would do two encores. Katarina…they all did encores. I got my money's worth. I wasn't paying them a heckuva lot, either."

What would become an enduring friendship between Boitano and Witt also began during those weeks and months.

During that tour, Witt skated to Michael Jackson's "Bad." One night, as the show ended and the skaters took their bows at center ice, Boitano and Witt looked up to see fans holding two signs.

One read: "Katarina, you are bad."

The other: "Brian, you are great."

Witt began crying.

Boitano was standing next to her. "Why are you crying?"

"How could they say this, that I am so bad and that you are so great?" Witt said. "I don't understand this."

Boitano shook his head.

"Katarina, you skate to the song 'Bad'. It means you're good, get it?"

"Oh," she said, "I get it now."

Brian Boitano said he thought the roof was going to "come off" when he was introduced for the first time as Olympic champion.

Boitano did more than translate signs on the 1988 tour. He also became the big brother of notorious tour cut-up Christopher Bowman.

"I was in charge of seeing that his bags were on the bus and he was on time and everything," Boitano said. "He was just such a wild man, it was really hard to watch over him. We were literally connected at the elbow. I was trying to be his father."

Bowman stories abound in tour lore and legend. There was the time he slept in the luggage hold of the bus because he had been out so late that he thought the only way not to miss the bus was to sleep in a place where everyone would find him.

Bowman, still a year away from becoming national men's champion, nearly missed the show's opening number in various cities because of his antics, Boitano said.

"We would get a five-minute call before the start of the show, and he would jump in the shower. Everyone else is ready, and he's just starting to get ready. He's in the shower. Then, sometimes he would be so late for the opening that he would have to crawl over the boards at the last minute and throw his guards at the wall and jump onto the ice for the opening. It was amazing."

She is "Bad": two-time Olympic gold medalist Katarina Witt (above) skated to Michael Jackson in 1988. Dancers Tracy Wilson and the late Rob McCall (left) won the Olympic bronze medal in their home country in 1988.

Jill Trenary (left), fourth at the Calgary Games, went on to win a world title in 1990. Although she did not give her best performance, Katarina Witt (above) edged Elizabeth Manley and Debi Thomas for the gold medal in Calgary.

Natalia Bestemianova and Andrei Bukin (right) rode onto the 1988 tour as four-time world ice dance champions and the Olympic gold medalists. Ever the class clown, Christopher Bowman (below) lived up to his nickname: "Bowman the Showman." Debi Thomas (below, right) was disappointed with her bronze medal at the 1988 Games but went on to a fine show career before becoming a doctor.

Shaving Cream in My Skates

SHE WAS PEGGY FLEMING, one of the most famous skaters of all time, but that didn't matter to Tom Collins and Paul Hendrickson on the final day of the 1991 tour.

"We have to do something funny. It's Peggy's last night," Collins whispered to Hendrickson backstage.

Fleming had agreed to skate on the tour to challenge herself just a few months before her 43rd birthday, to "see if I could do it again," but that lofty mission didn't matter anymore as Collins and Hendrickson cooked up their plan.

Fleming skated her number in an elegant, flowing gown, then came off the ice in the dark and quickly changed into a hat and long black opera gloves for an encore to "Ice, Ice Baby." It was Hendrickson's job to hold the gloves as Fleming put them on, place the hat on her head and push her back out.

"We had green Jell-O for dessert," Hendrickson told Collins. "I'm going to put Jell-O in her gloves. She'll jam her hand in and her glove will be filled with Jell-O."

Security director Lou McClary

"Great idea," Collins said. Then he thought for a moment: "No, we can't do that. We're going to wreck her dress. It's a $10,000 dress. She's going to get Jell-O all over."

"So what? It's the last night."

"No, no, no," Collins said. "I don't want to buy the dress."

"Okay, so what am I going to use?" Hendrickson considered his options. "We had oatmeal for breakfast. I'm going to use oatmeal."

"Great idea!" said Collins.

So as Fleming was preparing for her number, the boys were preparing for theirs.

"I cooked up the oatmeal and I poured it into her gloves," Hendrickson said. "Then I walked Peggy to the ice like I did every night. She went out for her number and everything was perfect, and her number ended and the crowd went crazy and she skated over to me."

He had the gloves open and ready. "She pushed her hand into the glove and she screamed bloody murder," Hendrickson said. "'Paul!' she yelled. I said, 'Peggy, you've got to put your other hand in. You've got to go. The music's playing.' She jammed her other hand in there and oatmeal was gushing out all over, clumps of it were falling out. I plopped the hat on her head and I turned her around and the music started. So she skated out, and this stuff is gooping out from her gloves, and she's shaking her hands and looking at me and everybody's laughing. Tommy's there laughing too."

"I remember it well," Fleming said with a smile. In her version of the story, however, the oatmeal never dripped out of her gloves.

"I knew, but the audience didn't," she said. "That was the point. Tom and Paul and the others were all standing there having a great laugh, but I still had to perform. That's the challenge of it. Then the fun thing is I get to get them back — but, come to think of it, I never got them back because that was the last show."

It's always the last show. The skaters pity the poor audience because the spectators have no idea what's going on. For her encore in 1992, Isabelle Brasseur skated with partner Lloyd Eisler to "Devil with the

Blue Dress," and, like Fleming, Brasseur had to make a quick change. Kristi Yamaguchi and Nancy Kerrigan always helped with the change. But on the last day of the tour, instead of putting on horns and a long tail, Yamaguchi and Kerrigan stuck on bunny ears and a cotton tail.

"I didn't know," Brasseur said. "I was on the ice and then I realized. I had to shake my tail — and there was no tail."

It happens every year. In addition to costume gags, there are numerous pranks, often involving shaving cream and champagne, not necessarily together.

"There's shaving cream in your skates," said Michelle Kwan, "and Dom Perignon being thrown everywhere. It's funny for the first bottle. Eight bottles later, I'm like, that's $800 right there."

If there was a man made for this moment, it was Christopher Bowman. The list of Bowman's antics is longer than the list of titles he won in Olympic-eligible skating. There's the time he was running late for the bus — and the next thing the other skaters knew, his clothes and bags were raining down upon them.

"I'm coming," Bowman yelled from his hotel room window as he tossed out all of his belongings.

Once on the bus, it didn't get easier for Bowman. One year, several of the women on the tour decided it would be funny to take off all of Bowman's clothes, with the exception of his underwear. Within minutes, the bus pulled up to the Four Seasons in San Francisco for the skaters to check in.

What was Bowman to do?

Undaunted, still wearing only his shorts, he snuck into the men's restroom in the lobby, wrapped himself like a mummy in toilet paper from head to toe and gingerly walked to the front desk to pick up his key.

Bowman also left an enduring legacy with a final-show prank one year in Dallas. Usually, one of the skaters will leave the rest of the troupe at center ice and go to the edge of the ice, pick up a wireless microphone and say a few words to acknowledge the last day of the tour. Bowman took this duty upon himself, then handed the microphone to Tom Collins and walked backstage.

No one gave him a second thought.

As the skaters stood on the ice and Collins thanked them and the audience, Bowman re-emerged with a fire hose — an old-fashioned, cloth fire hose. He yelled for an arena employee to turn on the water.

What happened next proves that Bowman had no idea how much pressure a fire hose packs.

He pointed the hose toward the skaters still on the ice.

"It just about blew everyone off their feet," Hendrickson said.

Fans in the first few rows of seats got soaked. The skaters scattered. Then the hose sprung a leak, flooding the backstage passageways.

"Christopher was not popular in Dallas after that," Hendrickson said.

Brian Boitano's pranks were not nearly as catastrophic.

His good friend Katarina Witt was traveling with her physical therapist, Oliver, who also did her laundry. One day, Oliver put Witt's workout pants in the dryer and shrunk them.

"Katarina never let him forget it," Boitano said. "She would scream, 'You shrunk these pants! You shrunk these pants!'"

Not long afterward, Boitano noticed that Witt had another pair of workout pants, which Oliver dutifully hung in the bus to dry.

"I snuck into the bus, took the pants and hemmed them with gaffer tape seven inches higher," Boitano said. "I taped them on the inside so she couldn't see the tape.

"Well, Katarina came in and she took one look at those pants and immediately screamed, 'Oliver!'

"It was great. Then I showed her what I had done and she said, 'Oh, okay.' But for a minute or two, she almost killed Oliver."

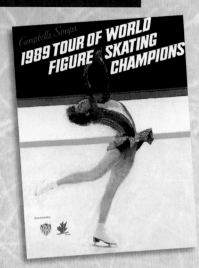

Campbell's Soups
1989 TOUR OF WORLD FIGURE SKATING CHAMPIONS

CAST OF SKATERS

1 Elena Bechke &
2 Denis Petrov, USSR
3 Brian Boitano, USA
4 Christopher Bowman, USA
5 Danny Doran, USA
6 Alexandr Fadeev, USSR
7 Karyn Garossino &
8 Rod Garossino, CANADA
9 Ekaterina Gordeeva &
10 Sergei Grinkov, USSR
11 Caryn Kadavy, USA
    Marina Klimova &
    Sergei Ponomarenko, USSR
12 Cindy Landry &
13 Lyndon Johnston, CANADA
14 Claudia Leistner, WEST GERMANY
15 Natalia Mishkutenok &
16 Artur Dmitriev, USSR
17 Brian Orser, CANADA

18 Viktor Petrenko, USSR
    Larisa Selezneva &
    Oleg Makarov, USSR
19 Natalie Seybold &
20 Wayne Seybold, USA
    Debi Thomas, USA
21 Jill Trenary, USA
    Maya Usova &
    Alexander Zhulin, USSR
22 Tracy Wilson &
23 Rob McCall, CANADA
24 Katarina Witt, EAST GERMANY
25 Susan Wynne &
26 Joseph Druar, USA

ALSO...

A Tom Collins
B Harris Collins
C Rudy Blinov
D Jan Claire
E David Sutton

1989

Russian dancers Marina Klimova and Sergei Ponomarenko (above) worked their way up from Olympic bronze in 1984 to Olympic silver in 1988 to, finally, Olympic gold in 1992. Two-time Olympic silver medalist Brian Orser (left) went on to a long career as a professional performer.

$\mathcal{T}$OM COLLINS KNEW it was time to make Champions on Ice an annual event. Spectators kept coming; in 1989, there was an average of 11,000 a night.

And the Russians kept coming, too. Artur Dmitriev, who would go on to win two Olympic gold medals with two different pairs partners, made his first appearance on the tour.

"This was the gold time of figure skating," he said, "1989 to 1994 or 1995. It couldn't have been better."

It was a good time for the Soviet pocket books as well. Prior to 1989, Collins had been paying a fee to the International Skating Union, which then would allow a few pennies to trickle down to the skaters. In 1989, Collins began paying the Soviet skating federation. Although the federation took much of the money, Collins believed a bit more went to the skaters.

"The kids were getting decent money," Collins said.

The tour was filled mostly with Olympic-eligible skaters, but Collins did have a core group of professionals around whom to build, including Brian Boitano, Brian Orser, Katarina Witt and 1988 Olympic bronze-medal-winning ice dancers Tracy Wilson and Rob McCall.

Each night, as Queen's "We Are the Champions" played in the arena and the troupe skated in a circle and waved to the crowd, the professionals would make up their own words: "We Are the Has-Beens."

"We had big smiles and we were waving and we were just singing along with our own words," Wilson said.

Even before she skated, Katarina Witt (below) created a stir at the Olympic Games — with her costume. There was never a dull moment with Christopher Bowman (below, left). In a crowd-pleasing move, he wore an Orioles jersey in Baltimore.

89

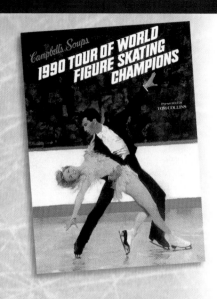

25 SHOWS IN 25 CITIES

BRIAN BOITANO WAS GONE, having left to tour on his own for a few years. But the tour, now established as a springtime mainstay for thousands who loved skating, continued unabated.

The Duchesnays, the exotic ice dancers from Canada who skated for France, joined up. "We wanted them after the 1988 Olympics," Tom Collins said, "and in 1989, we couldn't get them because they were doing various things in Europe and couldn't do the tour. I asked them to do their 1988 Olympic number, the African animal number."

Collins believed then and still does that the audience wants to see famous skaters do familiar numbers.

Rudy Galindo and Kristi Yamaguchi were on the tour, not as individuals but as a pair. They were the two-time U.S. national champions. "At that time, I don't think we realized what they were both going to become," Collins said.

It was their last year together as a pair, for Yamaguchi was forced to make a choice between singles and pairs, and she wisely chose to go it alone, moving on to the world title in 1991 and the Olympic gold medal in 1992. Galindo wouldn't resurface for six years, but when he did, it would become one of his sport's most enchanting moments.

CAST OF SKATERS

Jo-Ann Borlase &
Martin Smith, CANADA

Christopher Bowman, USA

Isabelle Brasseur &
Lloyd Eisler, CANADA

Kurt Browning, CANADA

Holly Cook, USA

Isabelle Duchesnay &
Paul Duchesnay, FRANCE

Todd Eldredge, USA

Ekaterina Gordeeva &
Sergei Grinkov, USSR

Midori Ito, Japan

Marina Klimova &
Sergei Ponomarenko, USSR

Cindy Landry &
Lyndon Johnston, CANADA

Natalia Lebedeva, USSR

Natalia Mishkutenok &
Artur Dmitriev, USSR

Mark Mitchell, USA

Viktor Petrenko, USSR

April Sargent &
Russ Witherby, USA

Jill Trenary, USA

Maya Usova &
Alexander Zhulin, USSR

Paul Wylie, USA

Susan Wynne &
Joseph Druar, USA

Kristi Yamaguchi &
Rudy Galindo, USA

Japan's Midori Ito was the greatest jumper in the history of women's skating; in 1998 in Nagano, she lit the Olympic cauldron.

Another pair who would stand the test of time with Champions on Ice emerged that year: Canadians Isabelle Brasseur and Lloyd Eisler.

"The big thing everyone looked forward to was you got to do show numbers, which you often didn't get to do during the year," Eisler said. "Back then, it was a way for us to make money and be able to pay for skating. There was no Grand Prix Series, no $300,000 a year to win.

"If you did really well during the year, Tommy invited you on this tour. It was kind of a bonus. You got to do it, got to see your friends, got to hone your craft a little more in front of the audience, and you got a chance to make enough money to continue the next year.

"Back in 1990, it was a game," Eisler added. "It was our play time. Twenty-five shows. It wasn't the be-all, end-all. It wasn't big business like it is now."

The Collins brothers — Harris in the team jacket and Tom on the right — were joined by a tuxedo-wearing Christopher Bowman, then-pairs partners Kristi Yamaguchi and Rudy Galindo, Paul Wylie and Gordeeva and Grinkov, among others.

Kristi Yamaguchi and Rudy Galindo (above) were two-time U.S. pairs champions, but Yamaguchi went solo in 1991 and won the Olympic gold medal in 1992. (Left) Kurt Browning, center, won the 1990 world title in Halifax, flanked by fellow medalists Viktor Petrenko and Christopher Bowman. Browning skated in several cities on the tour in 1988 and 1990.

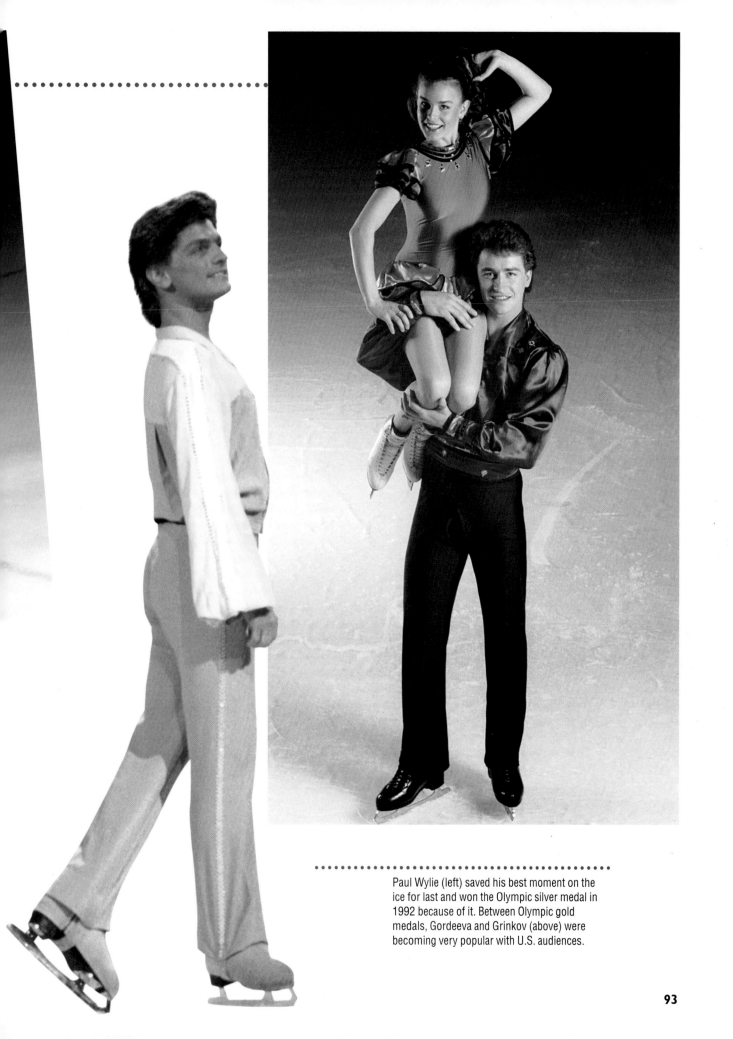

Paul Wylie (left) saved his best moment on the ice for last and won the Olympic silver medal in 1992 because of it. Between Olympic gold medals, Gordeeva and Grinkov (above) were becoming very popular with U.S. audiences.

History in Front of You Every Night

*I*T WAS THE SPRING OF 1991 and Peggy Fleming had it all. About to turn 43, she had the respect of several generations of sports fans, a wonderful family and career, and nothing left to prove, on the ice or off.

So what does she do? She joins skaters half her age on a 30-show skating tour, where with one false step, she could fall into the flowers or land in a heap on the ice. A most unusual decision, Fleming acknowledges, but she had her reasons.

"It was a challenge, a wonderful challenge," she said. "It was the challenge of doing the tour, the challenge of going out and skating like that again. It's good to fire yourself up, to scare yourself a little bit, especially as you get older. The challenge keeps you sharper when you're getting older. It's good to say 'Yes' to something different, to something new. You feel real good about yourself when you take on a new challenge and can do it. I wanted to see if I could do it again — and I could."

The 30 shows lasted six weeks. "I had a hard time being away from home. I had the family come in shifts. Our son Todd was just three years old then, and I had him join me in Phoenix, for example, where the tour stayed in a great hotel with a pool. Those were the kind of decisions we made."

For Fleming and her husband Greg Jenkins, a dermatologist, there was a method to this madness.

"It was good for my kids to know what Mom does," Fleming said. "Going from hotel to hotel, the long hours in the arena, the hours of practice, the bus rides, the autographs…it's a lot of work. They've been to Greg's office, too. It's good for your kids to know what Mom and Dad do. It's good to have that window on the world."

To many on the tour that year, Fleming had been untouchable. Some, like the skaters from the Soviet Union, had never seen her skate — even on television.

"I saw Peggy Fleming for the first time on that tour," said Artur Dmitriev. "I had never seen her before, ever, until the tour. Her moves, her arms, they were just unbelievable. I was in shock. I had heard about her but didn't understand why she was so popular until I saw her."

"It was like you were watching history in front of you every night," said production manager Paul Hendrickson

"To me, she's just the glamour of it all," said Jill Trenary. "So, then, it was interesting to see that she was just like us in a lot of ways — how nervous she gets, how she messes with her hair. She was one of us that year."

This was especially the case one night when Fleming breezed by Trenary on her way to the ice — and Trenary noticed a hairbrush caught in Fleming's flowing dress. Trenary reached down and grabbed it before Fleming hit the ice.

Fleming was well aware of how the other skaters might treat her, and she was thrilled when Kristi Yamaguchi and Trenary led a few other women in sunglasses onto the ice to mimic Fleming as she skated her encore at the end of the tour.

"I had a great laugh," Fleming said. "I'm not sure the audience knew what was going on, but it made me feel good that they felt comfortable having fun with me."

1991

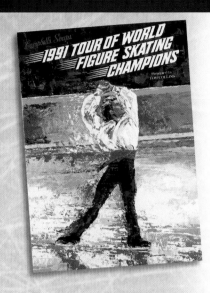

CAST OF SKATERS

Gary Beacom, CANADA

Elena Bechke &
Denis Petrov, USSR

Natalia Bestemianova &
Andrei Bukin, USSR

Christopher Bowman, USA

Isabelle Brasseur &
Lloyd Eisler, CANADA

Todd Eldredge, USA

Peggy Fleming, USA

Ekaterina Gordeeva &
Sergei Grinkov, USSR

Tonya Harding, USA

Nancy Kerrigan, USA

Marina Klimova &
Sergei Ponomarenko, USSR

Elizabeth Manley, CANADA

Natalia Mishkutenok &
Artur Dmitriev, USSR

Mark Mitchell, USA

Brian Orser, CANADA

Viktor Petrenko, USSR

Jill Trenary, USA

Barbara Underhill &
Paul Martini, CANADA

Maya Usova &
Alexander Zhulin, USSR

Elena Valova &
Oleg Vasiliev, USSR

Susan Wynne &
Joseph Druar, USA

Kristi Yamaguchi, USA

30 SHOWS IN 30 CITIES

*T*HIS YEAR WILL always be remembered in Champions on Ice lore and legend as the year Peggy Fleming joined the tour. She came on board just once, skated every show, and then was gone.

"Tommy twisted my arm," she said with a laugh.

Many skaters to this day fondly remember their opportunity to get to know the venerable Fleming as one of them.

"Peggy Fleming that year, Dorothy Hamill and Brian Boitano in other years," said Isabelle Brasseur. "Getting to know them on an everyday basis. You realize everyone is human."

But the getting-to-know-you process had its moments. "One day we were talking," said Jill Trenary, "and Peggy mentioned that she won the Olympics in 1968 and I said, 'Oh, that's the year I was born.'

"It just kind of came out. Ouch."

"I was older than everybody," Fleming said. "They could have been my kids, all of them."

The heirs apparent to Fleming as America's next ice princess were present all around her in the group photo.

"Kristi Yamaguchi, Nancy Kerrigan — and there's Tonya Harding," Tom Collins said. "What an array that is."

Collins remembered Harding as "the quietest person. She stayed by herself. She spent a lot of time in my office, just reading. She was kind of a loner — and never any problem at all."

Peggy Fleming wanted to challenge
herself at the ripe old age of 42, so she
joined the tour and skated every show.

Barbara Underhill and Paul Martini (left) , the 1984 world champions, went on to long careers on tour and in the television booth in their native Canada. Jill Trenary (below) was considered one of the most beautiful skaters of her day, and she soon would be helping young Michelle Kwan on tour.

Elizabeth Manley (below) parlayed one magical moment — her electric silver-medal-winning performance in Calgary — into a longtime show career. Brian Orser (left) became known as the consummate performer after his Olympic career ended. It was unprecedented in skating history — a 1-2-3 sweep by U.S. skaters Kristi Yamaguchi, Tonya Harding and Nancy Kerrigan (below left) at the 1991 worlds in Munich.

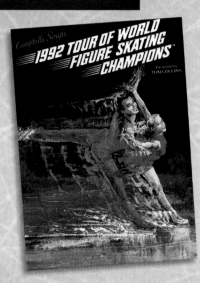

Campbells Soups
1992 TOUR OF WORLD FIGURE SKATING CHAMPIONS
Foreword by TOM COLLINS

CAST OF SKATERS

1 Peter Barna, CZECHOSLOVAKIA
2 Elena Bechke &
3 Denis Petrov, RUSSIA
4 Isabelle Brasseur &
5 Lloyd Eisler, CANADA
6 Lu Chen, CHINA
7 Oksana Grishuk &
8 Evgeny Platov, RUSSIA
9 Tonya Harding, USA
10 Nancy Kerrigan, USA
11 Marina Klimova &
12 Sergei Ponomarenko, RUSSIA
13 Radka Kovarikova &
14 Rene Novotny, CZECHOSLOVAKIA
15 Natalia Mishkutenok &
16 Artur Dmitriev, RUSSIA

17 Mark Mitchell, USA
18 Viktor Petrenko, UKRAINE
19 Jill Trenary, USA
20 Calla Urbanski &
21 Rocky Marval, USA
22 Maya Usova &
23 Alexander Zhulin, RUSSIA
24 Paul Wylie, USA
25 Kristi Yamaguchi, USA

ALSO...

A Tom Collins
B Harris Collins
C Elaine DeMore
D Paul Hendrickson
E Ming Su Lee
F Galina Zmievskaya
G David Sutton
H Don Watson

ANOTHER OLYMPIC YEAR, another 15,000 per city per night for Champions on Ice.

Olympic gold medalist Kristi Yamaguchi closed the show, but the men's Olympic gold medalist, Viktor Petrenko of the Ukraine, would be the one who stayed with Champions on Ice far longer.

After joining the tour in 1990, Petrenko, who defeated the popular American Paul Wylie in a controversial decision in Albertville, France, took his role very seriously. And that sounded funny coming from a man who thrived on kitschy comedy.

"Each time I step on the ice after winning the gold medal, I need to prove I deserve the title," Petrenko would say a decade later, still a mainstay on the tour. "Even now, I still feel like when I step on the ice, I have to prove I deserve being Olympic champion, even 10 years later."

One man who did not step on the ice at all — at least not for another two years — was Elvis Stojko, who finished third at the world championships in Oakland. Another mainstay-in-waiting for the tour, Stojko turned down Tom Collins' offer to join Champions on Ice so he could go back to his studies at York University in Toronto. He would join the tour in 1994.

Winner of the Olympic bronze medal in 1992, Nancy Kerrigan (right) became the top female skater in the United States when Kristi Yamaguchi (above) turned professional after winning her gold medal in Albertville.

Viktor Petrenko (left) won the Olympic gold medal in 1992 and says he wants to prove he deserves it every time he steps on the ice. Isabelle Brasseur and Lloyd Eisler (below, left) won the Olympic bronze medal in 1992 and again in 1994 and were on their way to a world title in 1993. Tonya Harding (below) is notorious for many reasons in figure skating, but was a quiet and reliable tour member.

Born in the USA

WHEN BRIAN BOITANO thinks back on his career, two moments stand out above all others.

"The end of the long program in the Olympics in Calgary," he said, "and when I was introduced for the first time as the Olympic champion on the tour in Cincinnati in 1988. I thought the roof was going to come off. 'Born in the USA' was part of the opening number. The lights were all off, and they did the first chords of Bruce Springsteen and then the lights popped on me and I was in my soldier outfit and I couldn't even move. I couldn't believe that the audience was so loud for me. I almost had to plug my ears."

Boitano starred in 12 summer tours and six winter tours of Champions on Ice. "The most dedicated skater I've ever had on the tour," Tom Collins calls him.

Collins' favorite Boitano program was "The Music of the Night," from *Phantom of the Opera*. "I would have done it every single year if Tommy would have had his way," Boitano said. "It was definitely a signature piece for me."

On one occasion during that 1989 tour, his luggage fell out of the bay of the bus on the highway, and his *phantom* costume was lost.

"Nobody called for a week and a half to say they found my luggage," Boitano said. "I was wondering, 'What are those people doing with my costume?' Eventually, I got it back."

Missing his outfit, Boitano wore a T-shirt and tights to perform that week. In the years to follow, Boitano adopted that style on the ice.

Year after year, Collins would try to persuade Boitano to bring back his *Phantom* program.

"He would say, 'I still get letters for that *Phantom of the Opera* number.' And I'd say, 'Oh, Tommy, let me have a life outside of *Phantom of the Opera*.'"

After his disappointing return to the Olympic Games in 1994, where he finished sixth, Boitano skated to another one of his favorite programs, Pavarotti's "Nessun Dorma."

"I didn't really want to go on tour because I didn't do well in the Olympics. I wondered, 'Maybe I shouldn't have done that, gone back.' I thought it might have ruined my popularity. But skating to 'Nessun Dorma,' it was the opposite reaction. They loved it. I realized, 'Gosh, it's almost like they like me better.' The crowds respect someone who goes through hardships and is up front about it, talks about it and is polite about it."

Then there was Boitano's robot costume. No one liked this one. It was way back in 1984 when Boitano debuted a program in which he skated as a robot. "I had lights going up and down my legs and arms, and sometimes the lights wouldn't work. I was constantly rewiring the costume."

In hindsight, he could have found easier costumes to wear. He had to keep buying new batteries because if one light went out, the entire circuit went out. And sometimes on a triple lutz, Boitano would get his arms tangled in the wires.

"He moved like a robot," Collins said, "and he skated like a robot and the sparks were flying from his costume and his skates. At the time, I doubted very much if Brian Boitano would go very far in figure skating."

When he retired from the tour in 2001, Boitano presented Collins with a surprise — the robot costume.

"I have it in my warehouse in Minneapolis," Collins said. "I go to the warehouse quite often, oddly enough, about once a week, and when I open the door, what's facing me? Brian Boitano's costume from that year. I just can't get away from it. It's with me all the time."

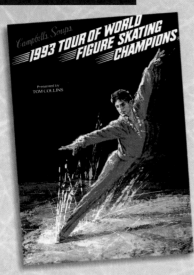

CAST OF SKATERS

1 Tai Babilonia &
2 Randy Gardner, USA
3 Oksana Baiul, UKRAINE
4 Peter Barna, CZECHOSLOVAKIA
5 Gary Beacom, CANADA
6 Brian Boitano, USA
  Surya Bonaly, FRANCE
7 Isabelle Brasseur &
8 Lloyd Eisler, CANADA
  Philippe Candeloro, FRANCE
9 Lu Chen, CHINA
20 Scott Davis, USA
11 Isabelle Duchesnay &
12 Paul Duchesnay, FRANCE
13 Nancy Kerrigan, USA
14 Marina Klimova &
15 Sergei Ponomarenko, RUSSIA
16 Jenni Meno &
17 Todd Sand, USA
18 Natalia Mishkutenok &

19 Artur Dmitriev, RUSSIA
20 Mark Mitchell, USA
21 Viktor Petrenko, UKRAINE
22 Jayne Torvill &
23 Christopher Dean, GREAT BRITAIN
24 Jill Trenary, USA
25 Calla Urbanski &
26 Rocky Marval, USA
27 Maya Usova &
28 Alexander Zhulin, RUSSIA

ALSO...

A Tom Collins
B Harris Collins
C Michael Collins
D Roger Bathurst
E Elaine DeMore
F Jon Drew
G Paul Hendrickson
H Ming Su Lee
I Dean Moyé
J Galina Zmievskaya
K David Sutton
L Don Watson

SKATERS WERE COMING BACK left and right for the 1994 Olympic Games, and so it was for Champions on Ice as well.

Brian Boitano was back. Torvill and Dean were back. Viktor Petrenko had never left the tour, but he was coming back in another way, making a tough decision to return for another Olympics. And Tai and Randy were back.

"I wanted some nostalgia in that show," Tom Collins said. "There was Tai and Randy, of course. And I had Torvill and Dean. They had not been with us since 1981. Now they were coming back because they wanted to get in front of the public before the Olympics."

"We were testing the waters to a certain degree," said Christopher Dean, who ended up meeting his wife, Jill Trenary, on the tour that year. "We put together a physical number [called "Drum Duet"] to see if we could still do it. After the tour, we were convinced we could."

Babilonia and Gardner had another reason for returning. In their 30's, they were not returning to the Games. This simply was their 25th anniversary together.

"Tommy didn't really need us because there are so many great skaters out there, the young whipper-snappers," Babilonia said, "but he was so great to let us celebrate that really special year on the tour. He didn't need us, but that's Tommy."

They skated to "I'll Be There" by Mariah Carey, with their voices mixed in speaking about their years together.

"The audience stood before we even started," Gardner remembered.

"They went nuts," Babilonia said. "They were happy to see us together again."

Sarah Kawahara choreographed their number; by the end of the decade, she would be working with the entire show.

As for Petrenko, he relied on Collins to help him make a difficult decision. With professionals allowed to reinstate for the Lillehammer Games, should he go back or protect his image and not chance it?

"He gave me advice and he was always right with what he told me," Petrenko said. "When I decided to turn from pro to amateur in 1993, the first person I called to ask was Tom. He said, 'You need to come back,' and that was enough. When you talk to a person like that, you have it settled in your mind. He said, 'No matter if you win or lose, it will be best for you,' and he was right."

Petrenko didn't win. He finished fourth, just ahead of Kurt Browning and Brian Boitano. The old veterans had a terrible Olympics. But Petrenko's star did not fall, at least not on Collins' tour. Not at all.

Nancy Kerrigan, the only 1992 Olympic women's medalist who would compete again in 1994, won the U.S. title in 1993.

Meanwhile, a couple of rising European stars with entirely different entertaining styles graced the ice for the first time on tour: Oksana Baiul and Philippe Candeloro.

Collins was in Prague when Baiul, then 15, captured an improbable world title.

He decided to help her, not only signing her for his tour but giving her financial assistance as well. He handed her $15,000, he said, "because she had nothing, these little beat-up skates, nothing else. She needed help."

Then there was Candeloro. "Paul Duchesnay was on the tour and he was talking about it back in France," he said. "I listened to him. I saw the book [program] from 1992, and I saw the many stars and many cities. I made a dream and in 1993, I was European medalist, and Tommy asked me and I came to the tour."

Passing the mantle of ice dancing innovation: from Torvill and Dean (left) to the brother-and-sister team of Paul and Isabelle Duchesnay (above).

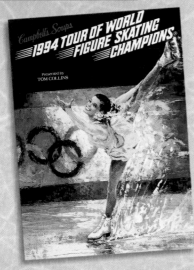

Campbell's Soups
1994 TOUR OF WORLD FIGURE SKATING CHAMPIONS
Presented by TOM COLLINS

CAST OF SKATERS

1 Oksana Baiul, UKRAINE
2 Gary Beacom, CANADA
3 Brian Boitano, USA
4 Surya Bonaly, FRANCE
5 Isabelle Brasseur &
6 Lloyd Eisler, CANADA
7 Philippe Candeloro, FRANCE
8 Lu Chen, CHINA
9 Scott Davis, USA
10 Isabelle Duchesnay &
11 Paul Duchesnay, FRANCE
12 Ekaterina Gordeeva &
    Sergei Grinkov, RUSSIA
13 Oksana Grishuk &
14 Evgeny Platov, RUSSIA
15 Nancy Kerrigan, USA
16 Marina Klimova &
17 Sergei Ponomarenko, RUSSIA
18 Michelle Kwan, USA
19 Jenni Meno &
20 Todd Sand, USA

21 Natalia Mishkutenok &
22 Artur Dmitriev, RUSSIA
23 Viktor Petrenko, UKRAINE
24 Elizabeth Punsalan &
25 Jerod Swallow, USA
26 Elvis Stojko, CANADA
27 Alexei Urmanov, RUSSIA
28 Maya Usova &
29 Alexander Zhulin, RUSSIA

ALSO...

A Tom Collins
B Harris Collins
C Michael Collins
D Marty Collins
E Roger Bathurst
F Suzanne Bonaly
G Jon Drew
H Paul Hendrickson
I Estella Kwan
J Linda Leaver
K Lou McClary
L Galina Zmievskaya
M David Sutton
N Paul Tillman

"*T*HE BIG YEAR," Tom Collins calls it.

"This was the biggest year ever for me, in every way, financially, people-wise. Near sell-outs in every city. It was an exciting show."

For the first time ever, Collins had to hire a security man for the show. With good reason. The attack on Nancy Kerrigan by associates of Tonya Harding at the U.S. national championships that January in Detroit had turned his sport into a soap opera and, by necessity, turned the backstage of every tour event into a very secure zone.

He brought in Lou McClary, who comes from a family of five generations of police officers in Southern California and had years of experience working with pro sports teams. McClary's job was to protect the skaters, especially Nancy Kerrigan.

Every night on tour, everyone had to wear or show their credential, called a laminant, to go anywhere backstage. There were no exceptions. Each year, the laminant featured a drawing of one of the skaters. Who was on the laminant for 1994?

Nancy Kerrigan, of all people.

One night on tour, Kerrigan was walking toward the dressing room. A security guard asked to see her credential.

She couldn't find it.

She searched and searched. She looked at him.

"Sorry ma'am, you need to have your laminant."

Exasperated, Kerrigan glared at him.

"I *am* the laminant!"

The guard let her pass.

McClary made it his job to make sure Kerrigan was taken care of at all times. Once that year, he dressed her in a hat and trench coat to sneak her past hundreds of fans in an arena. In his mind, it was just good police work.

Isabelle Brasseur roomed with Kerrigan on the tour that year. "It was really hard on her," Brasseur said. "She couldn't go out to the mall. She felt she had to stay in and stay away from people."

With all the star power that year, it would be easy to overlook the little girl on the left-hand side of the group photo.

But Collins doesn't.

"If you look closely," he says, "for the first time ever, Michelle Kwan."

She was still only 13, about to turn 14 that summer.

"Joining the tour is when you realize you have to become a show skater," Kwan said. "It was a big wake-up call, which was nice because I was able to learn quicker than somebody who hadn't experienced the tour or been around pro skaters."

Nancy Kerrigan survived the attack on her knee and the resulting firestorm of attention to win the silver medal at the Lillehammer Olympic Games.

Not your average male figure skater at 5-foot-7, Elvis Stojko (above right) rode dirt bikes, practiced martial arts and dressed casually on the ice. Fellow Canadians Brasseur and Eisler (above) weren't your average pair — but they didn't always dress as members of the opposite gender. Barely a teenager, Michelle Kwan (right) wasn't your average up-and-coming skater.

(Above) Gordeeva and Grinkov's 1994 Olympic long program, skated to Beethoven's "Moonlight Sonata," is considered a classic and was one of their last programs before Grinkov's 1995 death. Lu Chen (above, right) of China won the first of her two Olympic bronze medals in 1994. Surya Bonaly (right) never won an Olympic medal but did capture three world silver medals in the mid-1990s.

The men's competition at the 1994 Games was loaded, but it was little-known Alexei Urmanov (left) of Russia who won the gold medal. Elegant Oksana Baiul (below, left) was unknown when she won the 1993 world title. By 1994, at 16, she was the Olympic champion. (Below) Natalia Mishkutenok was Artur Dmitriev's partner when they won the 1992 Olympic gold medal and 1994 Olympic silver. They soon split, but Dmitriev wasn't finished yet.

Elvis Lives

AT THE 1992 WORLD championships in Oakland, it was clear that Elvis Stojko was about to become a very unorthodox superstar in the world of figure skating. He finished seventh at the Olympic Games in Albertville, France, then third at the worlds. Tom Collins believed the next logical step for Stojko was to join Champions on Ice.

"How would you like to do the tour?" Collins asked Stojko, then 20 years old.

"I'd be thrilled to do the tour," Stojko replied, "but I can't."

"Why?" Collins asked. He had never had any up-and-coming skater decline his offer.

"Well, I have to go back to university in Toronto," Stojko said.

Collins was dumbfounded. For a moment, he didn't know what to say.

"Elvis," he finally replied, "I can't believe what I'm hearing, but I love what I'm hearing. You go back to school. We'll talk again."

To this day, Collins and Stojko both enjoy telling this story now that Stojko is a cornerstone on Champions on Ice, and has been since 1994.

"He was so serious and I admired him so much," Collins said.

"He couldn't believe that I actually turned him down," said Stojko.

After returning to York University in Toronto, where he studied psychology, economics and even a little mythology, Stojko eventually decided that college was not for him. "I can't sit still in a class," he said. "I want to go and experience life in person, instead of through a book."

And so he did.

There was dirt-bike racing. There was auto racing. There were the martial arts. And there was skating,

very different, avant-garde figure skating.

"I've taken the sport in a new direction and opened it up to a lot more people," said Stojko, a three-time world champion. "I've been involved in other walks of life. I've been involved in the racing circuit, met a lot of people in the martial arts world. It's a bigger world than just skating; we're in this small world of skating, but we have to realize that there are other branches of life as well."

Stojko's size has dictated his role in skating. "I'm not 5-10, 5-11, and thin. I never did ballet. I'm never going to be like that. I'm 5-7, 168 pounds. I've skated to rock and roll, I've skated in jeans. I wanted to open up skating. I think I've done that."

With the retirement of Brian Boitano, Stojko has become the tour's most popular male skater.

"It's not my home country but people treat me like I'm from here," Stojko said. "I'm the adopted Canadian guy."

And, like Michelle Kwan, he is all the more beloved by audiences because he has come close to winning two Olympic gold medals, but has fallen short both times.

"Not winning the gold medal is a small part of me, but that's okay, I'll gladly give that up so that when I've left the sport, I'll be considered a legend in the sport," he said. "They can have the gold medal. But having legend status, not everyone gets that. To truly be a legend in the sport, to make a difference…there are people who come and go, champions who come and go. Who won that year? People forget.

"But you remember people for the things they've done and the way they've done them. I went about it my way. It was the right thing for me. It made me who I am and made a place for me in the sport that no one can take away."

CAST OF SKATERS

1 Oksana Baiul, UKRAINE
2 Nicole Bobek, USA
3 Brian Boitano, USA
4 Surya Bonaly, FRANCE
5 Isabelle Brasseur &
6 Lloyd Eisler, CANADA
7 Philippe Candeloro, FRANCE
8 Lu Chen, CHINA
9 Scott Davis, USA
10 Isabelle Duchesnay &
11 Paul Duchesnay, FRANCE
12 Todd Eldredge, USA
13 Oksana Grishuk &
14 Evgeny Platov, RUSSIA
15 Gia Guddat &
16 Gary Beacom, CANADA
17 Nancy Kerrigan, USA
18 Marina Klimova &
19 Sergei Ponomarenko, RUSSIA
20 Michelle Kwan, USA
21 Jenni Meno &
22 Todd Sand, USA
23 Viktor Petrenko, UKRAINE
24 Elizabeth Punsalan &
25 Jerod Swallow, USA
26 Renée Roca &
27 Gorsha Sur, USA
28 Elvis Stojko, CANADA
29 Jill Trenary, USA
30 Calla Urbanski &
31 Rocky Marval, USA
32 Maya Usova &
33 Alexander Zhulin, RUSSIA

ALSO...

A Tom Collins
B Harris Collins
C Michael Collins
D Roger Bathurst
E Doug Buss
F Elaine DeMore
G Jon Drew
H Elliott Harris
I Paul Hendrickson
J Lou McClary
K Dean Moyé
L Gene Siskel
M David Sutton
N Paul Tillman
O Don Watson

1995

Todd Eldredge (below), U.S. men's champion in 1990 and 1991 before being hampered by injury and illness, was on his way to a magnificent comeback in 1995, culminating in the 1996 world title. The husband-and-wife team of Sergei Ponomarenko and Marina Klimova (below, right) of Russia moved to Lake Arrowhead, Calif., to set up a professional career in America. Rocky Marval and Calla Urbanski (right) were a working class pair better known as "the Waitress and the Truck Driver."

$\mathcal{B}$Y 1995, CHAMPIONS ON ICE was still reaping the benefits of the Tonya/Nancy saga. There were more cities and shows than ever before. "This was the second biggest year in figure skating touring history," Tom Collins said. "We did more shows than in the Olympic year. In 1994, we had it booked a year or two before, so we really couldn't add anything. There were so many cities to play, it was unbelievable."

In the cast photo, taken in Chicago, the "thumbs up" might as well relate to the fortunes of figure skating at the time, although, in reality, the skaters posed that way in honor of movie critic Gene Siskel, who visited the tour and ended up joining the skaters for the photo.

The tour's youth movement continued as Nicole Bobek and Michelle Kwan, the top two finishers at the U.S. nationals that year, appeared on tour together.

"The first few years were tough, getting used to the ropes, how things go: This is when you eat. This is when you sleep. This is when your bag has to be out," Bobek said. "It's a schedule, it's a job. It's a job more than anything. It's a great job, but it does take time to adjust, to find your groove and then keep the performance level up and try to stay energetic throughout the day."

Kwan was learning too. She skated to a medley from *Peter Pan* that year, but even though she still was a young teenager, the tour wanted her to grow. Tour choreographer Harris Collins asked veteran Jill Trenary, in the last of her eight years on tour, to help Kwan in the opening number.

"Show her some moves, Tren," Harris said.

They worked together in practice for the opening number, Trenary trying to help not-yet-15-year-old Michelle play a "cutesy" part in the show's opening.

"She did a good job," Trenary said. "I can still see us on the ice, working together, Michelle and me, with Harris encouraging us."

On tour, there are no "illegal" skating moves, which meant an ice dance team like the Duchesnays could do just about anything.

CAST OF SKATERS

1 Oksana Baiul, UKRAINE
2 Nicole Bobek, USA
3 Brian Boitano, USA
  Surya Bonaly, FRANCE
4 Shae-Lynn Bourne &
5 Victor Kraatz, CANADA
6 Isabelle Brasseur &
7 Lloyd Eisler, CANADA
  Philippe Candeloro, FRANCE
8 Lu Chen, CHINA
9 Scott Davis, USA
10 Todd Eldredge, USA
11 Rudy Galindo, USA
12 Oksana Grishuk &
13 Evgeny Platov, RUSSIA
  Gia Guddat &
  Gary Beacom, CANADA
14 Dan Hollander, USA
15 Nancy Kerrigan, USA
16 Marina Klimova &
17 Sergei Ponomarenko, RUSSIA
18 Oksana Kazakova &
19 Artur Dmitriev, RUSSIA
20 Michelle Kwan, USA
21 Tonia Kwiatkowski, USA
22 Jenni Meno &
23 Todd Sand, USA
24 Eric Millot, FRANCE
25 Viktor Petrenko, UKRAINE
26 Elizabeth Punsalan &
27 Jerod Swallow, USA
28 Elvis Stojko, CANADA
29 Alexei Urmanov, RUSSIA

  Maya Usova &
30 Alexander Zhulin, RUSSIA
31 Mandy Woetzel &
32 Ingo Steuer, GERMANY

ALSO...

A Tom Collins
B Harris Collins chair
C Michael Collins
D Butch Collins
E Roger Bathurst
F Jana Bobek
G Doug Buss
H Jon Drew
I Elliott Harris
J Paul Hendrickson
K Estella Kwan
L Lou McClary
M Dean Moyé
N David Sutton
O Don Watson

When asked who they admire most on tour, the skaters invariably say one name: Brian Boitano (right). Dancers Liz Punsalan and Jerod Swallow (below), five-time U.S. champions, turned mature programs into an art form on tour.

*T*OM COLLINS FOUND the interest in his tour so great that he broke it into two parts. He created "the Winter Tour," as it's unofficially called, a smaller version of Champions on Ice, filled with professional skaters no longer in the Olympic division. The tour played 15 to 20 smaller cities in January and February while the Olympic-eligible skaters were busy competing.

"We were doing so many cities that it was too much for the skaters," Collins said. "During the tour in 1995, I said, 'We're doing 76 shows; we're running into July, it's getting so late. We have to break this show up.'"

The decision allowed Collins to bring in one of the sport's greatest legends: Dorothy Hamill. About to turn 40, Hamill had been thinking of giving up skating entirely after dealing with personal and financial crises involving her ownership of Ice Capades.

Then came Collins' phone call. "Joining Tommy's tour was a breath of fresh air," she said. "It made skating pleasurable again."

Some, such as Brian Boitano, participated in both the winter and summer tours. One who rejoined the summer tour after resurrecting his career was Rudy Galindo, whose stunning victory at the 1996 U.S. nationals in his hometown of San Jose, Calif., led to a multi-year deal with Champions on Ice.

The poignancy of the team picture in 1996 is unmistakable. The empty director's chair belonged to Harris Collins, the creative heart and soul of the tour, who died June 1 of a heart attack backstage before the first of the tour's two shows in Chicago. He was 49.

Harris, who had joined the tour in 1975 as a creative sounding board for his brother, was beloved by many of the skaters. He took young Michelle Kwan under his wing. He was a friend to everyone and a mainstay on tour.

Harris was about to give the five-minute call to the skaters when he fell on the rugs just inside the backstage curtain. Two paramedics ran over, realized he had not simply tripped and began to work furiously on him. Paul Hendrickson and Michael Collins, who had been within a few feet of Harris when he fell, feared the worst. "I knew something was very wrong because he didn't move," Hendrickson said.

He and Collins then made one of the most difficult decisions of their careers. "There are thousands of people out there in the audience," they said. "We have to start the show."

The situation was awful. There was another show in the evening, so the skaters didn't find out what had happened to Harris Collins until after the second show. "Harris had a heart attack and died instantly," Michael Collins told them. "We wanted to tell you, but we knew we couldn't until after the shows. He died around us, among the people he loved the most."

(Above) The late Harris Collins had been a vital and respected member of Champions on Ice since 1975.

(Left) Rudy Galindo's heart-warming U.S. title led to an invitation to join the tour, which led to a successful career as a professional skater.

Always delighted to work with skaters on tour, Harris Collins joins dancers Maya Usova and Alexander Zhulin on the ice (left).

A Legend Returns

*T*HERE WAS A TIME when Dorothy Hamill thought she might never perform again.

It was the mid-1990s. Her highly publicized ownership of Ice Capades was in a shambles. Her marriage was coming to an end. The sport that had given her so much over the past 20 years was making her life miserable.

"I was never going to skate again," Hamill said.

Then, Tom Collins decided to start his winter tour of Champions on Ice in 1996. He called Hamill to see if she was interested. The offer was intriguing to her. She wouldn't have to run the tour, pay salaries, organize anything.

She would just have to skate, and Dorothy Hamill certainly knew how to do that.

"The greatest thing was that after this horror story of my personal life, joining Tommy's tour was a breath of fresh air," Hamill said. "I didn't have to worry about anything involving the tour. I only had to be concerned with four minutes on the ice, with my costume and my music. Everything else was being taken care of. There was no pressure at all.

"I had gotten to the point where I didn't enjoy skating anymore. This gave me a new love of skating again. It had been such a big part of my life, but I ended up hating it. Then to join Tommy's tour, it lightened the load. It made skating pleasurable again."

Hamill, now 46, has skated on every winter tour since 1996, seven in all heading into 2003. She also has skated on three summer tours: 1975 and portions of the 1997 and 2000 tours.

The response from audiences to Hamill's return has been extraordinary. Everywhere she goes, spectators invariably give her the evening's warmest ovation.

"It always surprises me so much and embarrasses me," she said. "It's warm and very wonderful and something I just never expected. I don't understand it, but it usually brings a tear to my eye."

Her fellow skaters treat her with a similar reverence.

"From the time she comes through the curtain, skates, bows, leaves the ice and goes back through the curtain, if you want to learn anything about performing and being professional, you should watch Dorothy," said ice dancer Jerod Swallow.

Hamill spends very little time dwelling on her 1976 Olympic gold medal. She didn't have a videotape of her performance from the Innsbruck Olympic Games for the longest time, until a friend at ABC Sports sent her one. Then, when she popped it in with her daughter and other family members a few years ago, they all enjoyed a good laugh.

"I absolutely cringed," Hamill said. "Oh my God, that was awful."

Dorothy Hamill?

Awful?

"It's not the greatest I've ever done," Hamill replied with a laugh. "I had a little trip at the end of my program. I was slightly off-balance. I notice that when I watch the tape."

Hamill, who admits to having been "painfully shy" during the mid-1970s when she first gained her fame, said that even now, she is not entirely certain why she is so beloved.

"I've never been confident receiving applause," she said. "I'm just a dumb ice skater. I tell everyone I just happen to do something I really love. I don't get why people react the way they do, but it's thrilling, and I do appreciate it. I really do."

61 SHOWS IN 59 CITIES

CAST OF SKATERS

1 Oksana Baiul, UKRAINE
2 Gary Beacom, CANADA
3 Nicole Bobek, USA
4 Brian Boitano, USA
5 Surya Bonaly, FRANCE
6 Shae-Lynn Bourne &
7 Victor Kraatz, CANADA
8 Isabelle Brasseur &
9 Lloyd Eisler, CANADA
10 Philippe Candeloro, FRANCE
11 Todd Eldredge, USA
12 Rudy Galindo, USA
13 Oksana Grishuk &
14 Evgeny Platov, RUSSIA
15 Vanessa Gusmeroli, FRANCE
16 Oksana Kazakova &
17 Artur Dmitriev, RUSSIA
18 Nancy Kerrigan, USA
19 Marina Klimova &
20 Sergei Ponomarenko, RUSSIA
   Ilia Kulik, RUSSIA
21 Michelle Kwan, USA
22 Tara Lipinski, USA
23 Jenni Meno &
24 Todd Sand, USA
25 Viktor Petrenko, UKRAINE
26 Elizabeth Punsalan &
27 Jerod Swallow, USA
28 Elvis Stojko, CANADA
29 Laurent Tobel, FRANCE
30 Calla Urbanski &
31 Rocky Marval, USA
   Alexei Urmanov, RUSSIA
32 Maya Usova &
33 Alexander Zhulin, RUSSIA

34 Mandy Woetzel &
35 Ingo Steuer, GERMANY

ALSO…

A Tom Collins
B Michael Collins
C Marty Collins
D Butch Collins
E Roger Bathurst
F Jana Bobek
G Suzanne Bonaly
H Doug Buss
I Elaine DeMore
J Eddie Einhorn
K Randy Gardner
L Paul Hendrickson
M Eric Lang
N Pat Lipinski
O Lou McClary
P Tamara Moskvina
Q Dean Moyé
R Nina Petrenko
S Irene Stojko
T David Sutton

Tai Babilonia and Randy Gardner (right) celebrated their 25th anniversary on the ice in 1993, then skated on the Champions on Ice winter tour for several years. Shae-Lynn Bourne and Victor Kraatz (below) display one of their characteristic power moves.

WOMEN HAVE ALWAYS been the stars of figure skating, and so it had become with Champions on Ice. A new star emerged on the tour in 1997: Tara Lipinski. She had upset Michelle Kwan at the U.S. nationals and the world championships, so she joined Kwan as one of Tom Collins' headliners leading into the Nagano Olympics.

Randy Gardner was back with the summer tour, not as a performer but as choreographer of the opening and closing numbers after the death of Harris Collins. "It was wonderful to be working with all that talent," Gardner said.

Gardner and Tai Babilonia were back on the ice on the winter tour, skating for two more seasons, 1997 and 1998.

This was a difficult year for Nicole Bobek, America's other Olympic contender. Her coach Carlo Fassi died of a heart attack during the 1997 world championships in Lausanne, Switzerland. Without Fassi, Bobek began to lean more on Tom Collins.

"For me, he's like another Carlo," Bobek said. "In 1997, he got me a car so I could get to the rink in Lake Arrowhead. When you need a helping hand, when something's wrong, Tommy will be there."

Canadian Gary Beacom (above) brought his innovative and humorous "I'm Your Man" program to the tour. Todd Sand and Jenni Meno (left), three-time world medalists, became husband and wife off the ice.

CAST OF SKATERS

Marina Anissina &
Gwendal Peizerat, FRANCE

Oksana Baiul, UKRAINE

1 Elena Berezhnaya &
2 Anton Sikharulidze, RUSSIA

3 Nicole Bobek, USA

4 Surya Bonaly, FRANCE

Shae-Lynn Bourne &
Victor Kraatz, CANADA

Isabelle Brasseur &
Lloyd Eisler, CANADA

5 Maria Butyrskaya, RUSSIA

Philippe Candeloro, FRANCE

Lu Chen, CHINA

6 Todd Eldredge, USA

7 Rudy Galindo, USA

8 Pasha Grishuk &
9 Evgeny Platov, RUSSIA

10 Oksana Kazakova &
11 Artur Dmitriev, RUSSIA

12 Nancy Kerrigan, USA

13 Marina Klimova &
14 Sergei Ponomarenko, RUSSIA

15 Anjelika Krylova &
16 Oleg Ovsiannikov, RUSSIA

17 Ilia Kulik, RUSSIA

18 Michelle Kwan, USA

19 Tonia Kwiatkowski, USA

20 Tara Lipinski, USA

21 Jenni Meno &
22 Todd Sand, USA

23 Viktor Petrenko, UKRAINE

24 Evgeni Plushenko, RUSSIA

25 Elizabeth Punsalan &
26 Jerod Swallow, USA

27 Irina Slutskaya, RUSSIA

1998 Tour

Elvis Stojko, CANADA

28 Laurent Tobel, FRANCE

Alexei Urmanov, USSR

29 Maya Usova &
30 Alexander Zhulin, RUSSIA

Michael Weiss, USA

Mandy Woetzel &
Ingo Steuer, GERMANY

ALSO...

A Tom Collins
B Michael Collins
C Marty Collins
D Butch Collins
E Roger Bathurst
F Doug Buss
G Elaine DeMore
H Jon Drew
I Paul Hendrickson
J Eric Lang
K Rocky Marval
L Lou McClary
M Ron Russell
N David Sutton

*T*HE OLYMPIC GAMES were over, and it was Tara Lipinski, not Michelle Kwan, who was closing the show by virtue of winning the gold medal in Nagano.

But there was no doubt who drew the warmest applause.

"Michelle has always been so beloved," Tom Collins said. "The audience loves Michelle. It's longevity. What other skater has had so many years at the very top of the sport?"

Two Russians who were going to be heard from again appeared on tour for the first time: Irina Slutskaya and Evgeni Plushenko.

"We heard about Evgeni, this new guy from Russia," Collins said. "I thought it would be good to have him on tour."

Said tour performance director Brian Klavano: "Tommy provides an outlet for kids. Plushenko has been in the show since 1998. That was before he really stepped up to the plate. Tommy recognizes that talent. He had Michelle in the show long before she was Michelle Kwan. Liz Manley can remember being in the show when she was 11 years old; she had a little novice title somewhere and Tommy let her skate with the show in Ottawa near her hometown, and that marked her. She said, 'Oh my God, I got to be on the ice with all those stars.'"

The tour was an oasis of sorts after the long Olympic season.

"It was the first time we had seen the sun in eight months," said ice dancer Liz Punsalan, who with her husband Jerod Swallow finished seventh at the Olympic Games. "And we finally got to spend time with our friends. As an amateur, you're always traveling with them but competing against them, so you're under stress and you don't really get to know them. As amateurs, we all have blinders on. We have known of each other for 10 years or so, as competitors, but we never really got to know each other until we got on tour."

Olympic silver medalists in 1994, Russians Maya Usova and Alexander Zhulin brought their elegant skating to the tour.

Powerful Michael Weiss
(above) made his first Olympic
team in 1998 and won U.S.
titles in 1999 and 2000. Four
marvelous minutes on the ice in
Nagano changed the life of
15-year-old Olympic gold
medalist Tara Lipinski.

1998

(Above) She became known only as Pasha after dropping her given name, Oksana Grishuk. He remained Evgeny Platov. Together they won two Olympic gold medals. Nicole Bobek (left), a showgirl at heart, left the Olympic ranks and turned professional after a disappointing performance in Nagano at the 1998 Olympics.

There was no telling what Philippe Candeloro (right) would try next on tour, while Ilia Kulik (below) brought his breathtaking jumps to Champions on Ice after winning the Olympic gold medal.

Tears of Joy, Tears of Sadness

*T*HE FIRST TIME THE figure skating world cried with Rudy Galindo, it shed tears of joy. That was January 1996, and a roaring crowd of 10,869 was on its feet in his hometown of San Jose. No one could believe their eyes: Galindo, so poor he lived in a trailer park and had to ride a bicycle to practice, so disenchanted with his career that he had quit skating for eight months, had won the U.S. men's national figure skating championship.

The moment Galindo finished skating, he lifted his eyes to the rafters: "Thank you, Dad! Thank you, George, Jim, Rick!"

They were the most important men in his life, and they all were dead: his father, his big brother, George, and coaches Jim Hulick and Rick Inglesi. All but his father died of complications related to AIDS.

The skating world cried again with Galindo on April 5, 2000, but these were tears of sadness because that was the day he announced that he, too, was HIV-positive.

"I sometimes ask myself, 'Why has this happened to me?'" Galindo said at the time. "I took care of my brother and saw every day what he went through, and that was a nightmare, although I know he didn't take care of himself. And I think of that sometimes, but then I tell myself that it's different now, that the medicine is better and that I am very different from my brother. Still, you don't think it's going to happen to you, and now it has."

Diagnosed with HIV on March 1, 2000, after contracting pneumonia while performing on the Champions on Ice winter tour, Galindo did not want to stop skating. He was scheduled to take part in the 36-show summer tour, which began in early April, and Tom Collins encouraged him to do so.

"It didn't bother me for a second that he had HIV," Collins said. "He's a great person, a great skater, a trooper. I told him that this illness is something we will have to live with. Not just Rudy Galindo, but all of us on the tour. I told him, 'You are with us no matter what, Rudy.'"

But Galindo, then 30, wasn't sure what he could endure. "I asked my doctor, 'Am I going to be able to tour again? Am I going to be able to skate?' I just remember the days of my brother dying and so I thought I was going to die. But my doctor told me that he had friends with HIV who were running marathons. I didn't believe him — until the tour started and I began skating every night."

Galindo and his sister Laura, who is his coach and best friend, chose the poignant "Send in the Clowns" for Galindo's number that year. The applause was overwhelming. It confirmed for them that Galindo's greatest medicine was simply getting on with his life, and that meant skating.

"I was taking my medication: three pills at night and one in the morning," he said. "Except for taking a couple of days off for blood work, I did the whole tour. By being on the tour, it really confirmed for me that my doctor was right. This is not a death sentence. You can be very productive in life. By skating on the tour, I learned I could still be a strong person and live a normal life."

50 SHOWS IN 45 CITIES

CAST OF SKATERS

1 Marina Anissina &
2 Gwendal Peizerat, FRANCE
3 Oksana Baiul, UKRAINE
4 Elena Berezhnaya &
5 Anton Sikharulidze, RUSSIA
6 Nicole Bobek, USA
7 Brian Boitano, USA
8 Surya Bonaly, FRANCE
  Shae-Lynn Bourne &
  Victor Kraatz, CANADA
  Maria Butyrskaya, RUSSIA
  Philippe Candeloro, FRANCE
9 Todd Eldredge, USA
10 Rudy Galindo, USA
11 Timothy Goebel, USA
12 Oksana Kazakova &
13 Artur Dmitriev, RUSSIA
14 Marina Klimova &
  Sergei Ponomarenko, RUSSIA
  Anjelika Krylova &
  Oleg Ovsiannikov, RUSSIA
15 Michelle Kwan, USA
16 Elizabeth Manley, CANADA
  Naomi Nari Nam, USA
17 Viktor Petrenko, UKRAINE
  Evgeni Plushenko, RUSSIA
18 Elizabeth Punsalan &
19 Jerod Swallow, USA
20 Elvis Stojko, CANADA
21 Laurent Tobel, FRANCE
22 Alexei Urmanov, RUSSIA
  Maya Usova &
  Evgeny Platov, RUSSIA
23 Michael Weiss, USA

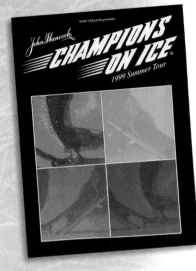

Mandy Woetzel &
Ingo Steuer, GERMANY
Alexei Yagudin, RUSSIA

ALSO...

A Tom Collins
B Marty Collins
C Butch Collins
D Roger Bathurst
E Suzanne Bonaly
F Doug Buss
G Elaine DeMore
H Jon Drew
I Jim Ellis
J Paul Hendrickson
K Brian Klavano
L Eric Lang
M Lou McClary
N Lynn Plage
O Grant Rorvick
P Ron Russell
Q David Sutton
R David Wingart

With a new haircut and the same magnificent spiral, Michelle Kwan continued to be the most dominant figure skater on earth, winning the world championships in 1998, 2000 and 2001.

THE YEAR AFTER the Olympic Games is often a crossroads in a skater's career. Nicole Bobek made the decision to leave the Olympic world and turn to the show-style, professional world, even though there were very few pro competitions remaining on the skating landscape.

"I was really afraid that Tommy wouldn't want me if I turned pro, but that wasn't the case at all," she said. "I called him and said, 'I don't know if I want to go another four years [to the Salt Lake City Olympics],' and he said, 'Well, there's your answer. You're a performer, you're great, you're musical. You do your show stuff and I want you. You're on the tour.'

"That was so great to hear."

While Bobek made a career-altering decision, young Timothy Goebel was just beginning his climb into the upper reaches of skating. And to do that, he had to work on his presentation skills.

He began focusing more on choreography with his competitive programs, and he did the same with the tour.

"Every night you have to get out and perform, and sometimes you don't feel that great, but you still want to get the crowd's reaction to the skating, and not necessarily with the jumps," Goebel said. "A lot of times with no warm-up and no practice you can't really do your most difficult elements. So you have to focus on presentation."

That, Goebel knew, was going to become his greatest challenge.

"Entertaining the audience is a different mind set. In a show, it's nice to take a break and focus on something else, but I think now is the time to make both work together. This tour is a proving ground. Judges and different skating officials are coming to these shows and seeing me in a different light, out of competition. Once someone gets a certain perception of someone in competition, it's very hard to get them to change that. I think if they see some changes in an exhibition setting, then they're going to be more responsive to really paying attention to what I'm doing on the ice in competition."

Goebel was not the only skater taking the first big steps into exhibition skating. Sarah Hughes, then 14, joined Champions on Ice for three shows near her New York home.

Michelle Kwan with mentor and close friend Brian Boitano.

Tom Collins brought professionals aboard in earnest in the 1980s. By the end of the 1990s, many were tour mainstays. They include Artur Dmitriev and new partner Oksana Kazakova (above), winners of the 1998 pairs Olympic gold medal, and Olympic stars (left to right) Oksana Baiul, Philippe Candeloro and Elizabeth Manley. Leading the tour's array of Olympic-eligible skaters was Michelle Kwan (far right).

"One Big Hug"

*T*HERE WAS A TIME WHEN Michelle Kwan blocked out the crowd on the Champions on Ice tour.

"Sometimes people say, 'Wow, did you hear that audience?' And I didn't; sometimes I put it on mute. But this year, I said, 'What am I doing?' and I took it off mute."

And then what happened?

"It was like one big hug," said Kwan. "It was so nice. I told myself, 'I've got to enjoy it. This isn't going to last for a very long time, so soak it up and cherish it.'"

Kwan continued: "I've always appreciated it, but it's hitting closer to home, maybe because I'm getting older and realizing there are other things in life and that later on, you will move on. I'm like, 'Oh, I'm going to miss this.' Especially when you think that we're on tour for four months. That's a big chunk of your life, being on the road.

"Then suddenly you're home and you'll be bored and you'll wish you were on tour and visiting great cities and staying in great hotels and being treated first-class again."

The 2002 tour was especially meaningful for Kwan, the sentimental favorite who ended up finishing third at the Salt Lake City Olympic Games.

"I don't know how many millions of people watched the Olympics, but then they want to see you," she said. "That's why they come to the show, not necessarily to see you do a triple jump, but they just want to see you, see you live after the Olympics.

"For me, when they see me, they know what I've gone through and they know my story and they understand. I wouldn't say it's a lovefest, but it's, 'Oh, there's Michelle….' I think people were rooting for me during the Olympics, and through the years, the last Olympics as well. They've seen me on TV at the nationals and worlds, and for me to be in every city and for people to be able to buy tickets and know the tour's coming to their town, it's nice because I can get closer and closer to them."

Although she's only 22, Kwan has been on tour for nine seasons, going back to 1994 when she finished second in the United States and eighth at the world championships.

"Every arena I go to now on tour, I have memories," she said. "I say, 'This is Boston. This is where I won nationals in 2001. Cleveland: the nationals the year before.' I can go down the list: Providence, Philadelphia, Salt Lake City in 1999, even going back to Orlando, where I competed in my first nationals in 1992. Everywhere I go, there are memories there for me now."

And there are memories for others as well.

"I would go out and watch her every night," close friend Brian Boitano said of Kwan's early years on tour. "I felt simpatico with her. For a young girl, she was very in touch with how to perform and how to approach the performance. I noticed a lot of me in her when she was young. She was doing this Peter Pan thing and I would go and watch her every night. And I would love watching her because she was just so cute. She had so much feeling and so much spunk, even at that age."

Tom Collins has also watched her grow up in front of his eyes.

"She's handled it so well: the ups in her career and especially the downs," he said. "If that were me, I would scream. I would be a basket case. To handle what's happened to her at the Olympics with class and dignity even as she must be hurting inside, that really impresses me."

2000

36 SHOWS IN 34 CITIES

CAST OF SKATERS

Marina Anissina &
Gwendal Peizerat, FRANCE

Oksana Baiul, UKRAINE

1 Elena Berezhnaya &
2 Anton Sikharulidze, RUSSIA
3 Vladimir Besedin &
4 Oleksiy Polishchuk, RUSSIA
5 Nicole Bobek, USA
6 Brian Boitano, USA
7 Surya Bonaly, FRANCE
8 Shae-Lynn Bourne &
9 Victor Kraatz, CANADA
10 Isabelle Brasseur &
11 Lloyd Eisler, CANADA
   Maria Butyrskaya, RUSSIA
12 Philippe Candeloro, FRANCE
   Sasha Cohen, USA
13 Todd Eldredge, USA
14 Rudy Galindo, USA
15 Timothy Goebel, USA
16 Dorothy Hamill, USA
17 Dan Hollander, USA
   Sarah Hughes, USA
18 Oksana Kazakova &
19 Artur Dmitriev, RUSSIA
20 Marina Klimova &
21 Sergei Ponomarenko, RUSSIA
22 Michelle Kwan, USA
23 Naomi Nari Nam, USA
24 Viktor Petrenko, UKRAINE
25 Evgeni Plushenko, RUSSIA
26 Elizabeth Punsalan &
27 Jerod Swallow, USA
28 Jamie Sale &
29 David Pelletier, CANADA

30 Elvis Stojko, CANADA
31 Maya Usova &
32 Evgeny Platov, RUSSIA
33 Michael Weiss, USA
   Alexei Yagudin, RUSSIA

ALSO...

A Tom Collins
B Michael Collins
B Butch Collins
D Roger Bathurst
E Suzanne Bonaly
F Zane Collings
G Elaine DeMore
H Jon Drew
I Jim Ellis
J Paul Hendrickson
K Brian Klavano
L Eric Lang
M Lou McClary
N Dean Moyé
O Grant Rorvick
P Ron Russell
Q David Sutton
R Paul Tillman
S Jeff Wendt

. . . .

*A*S THE SKATING WORLD built toward an Olympic Games on U.S. ice, so too did Champions on Ice. Future Olympic stars Elena Berezhnaya and Anton Sikharulidze and Jamie Sale and David Pelletier appeared on the tour, perhaps foreshadowing their future connection in the annals of skating history.

It must be noted that there was no French judge nearby to cause any controversy when they skated on the tour.

Another future starlet was tapped and invited to come aboard for 2000. She had appeared in one show in 1999.

"Sasha Cohen was invited when she was a little Miss Maybe," said tour performance director Brian Klavano. "Now she's a contender. I truly think being invited to be on Tommy's show, just in your hometown, then around the country, makes you believe."

The tour's cast ran the gamut from the promise of Sasha Cohen to the legend of Dorothy Hamill. Then 43, Hamill had been performing to warm ovations on the winter tour, but Tom Collins wanted her to be seen by a wider audience. That idea was soon curtailed by an injury.

After opening the show in Baltimore, the tour went to Washington, where the show's TV special was being taped. Although she had skated that day, Hamill did not have a chance to warm up before the opening number — and strained her hip flexor doing a flying spin. "When you're my age, you need that warm-up," Hamill said.

Hamill missed several shows, then prepared a number skated to Louis Armstrong that included no jumps or spins. "And I got a standing ovation the first show," she said. "That was very strange to me. I didn't do anything for two minutes, but I got a standing ovation."

In the last handful of cities, Hamill returned to her original number, skated to Patti LuPone, which featured a couple of double jumps. She received standing ovations then as well.

The tour's tradition of ending the final show with a series of pranks — a ritual that was near and dear to Brian Boitano's heart — continued unabated. As the tour's *Bolero* finale ended the last night of the 2000 tour, Boitano became the target of an extensive pie-throwing onslaught. Michael Weiss and Elvis Stojko led the way, chasing Boitano around the rink with shaving-cream pies as the crowd, which had been filing out, stopped in its tracks, turned around, and began yelling, "Get him! Get him!"

"We were racing all around the ice," Weiss said. "The audience loved it. I got him in the face. The audience must have been wondering what in the world was going on, but they loved it."

"He didn't get me," Boitano protested. "He threw it and it missed me and I picked it up and got him."

. . . .
Brian Boitano was nearing the end of his touring career with Champions on Ice in 2000.

Dorothy Hamill (above) joined the summer tour, only to injure her hip flexor and miss several shows. Rudy Galindo (right) announced he was HIV-positive in April 2000 but joined the tour for the first show and skated for all but a few shows that year.

2000

152

(Clockwise from far left) Liz Punsalan and
Jerod Swallow, Evgeni Plushenko, Elena
Berezhnaya and Anton Sikharulidze,
Michael Weiss and Michelle Kwan.
(Overleaf) For group numbers, costume
designer Pete Menefee first sketches
then constructs each skater's costume.
These were worn for the tour's opening
number in 2000.

22 SHOWS IN 20 CITIES

CAST OF SKATERS

1 Elena Berezhnaya &
2 Anton Sikharulidze, RUSSIA
3 Vladimir Besedin &
4 Oleksiy Polishchuk, UKRAINE
5 Nicole Bobek, USA
6 Brian Boitano, USA
7 Surya Bonaly, FRANCE
8 Isabelle Brasseur &
9 Lloyd Eisler, CANADA
10 Philippe Candeloro, FRANCE
  Sasha Cohen, USA
11 Todd Eldredge, USA
12 Rudy Galindo, USA
13 Timothy Goebel, USA
14 Dan Hollander, USA
  Sarah Hughes, USA
15 Oksana Kazakova &
16 Artur Dmitriev, RUSSIA
17 Michelle Kwan, USA
18 Viktor Petrenko, UKRAINE
19 Evgeni Plushenko, RUSSIA
20 Elizabeth Punsalan &
21 Jerod Swallow, USA
22 Jamie Sale &
23 David Pelletier, CANADA
24 Irina Slutskaya, RUSSIA
25 Elvis Stojko, CANADA
26 Maya Usova &
27 Evgeny Platov, RUSSIA
28 Michael Weiss, USA

ALSO...

A Tom Collins
B Michael Collins
C Butch Collins
D Mark Collins
E Roger Bathurst
F Suzanne Bonaly
G Zane Collings
H Elaine DeMore
I Jon Drew
J Paul Hendrickson
K Brian Klavano
L Eric Lang
M Lou McClary
N Dean Moyé
O Grant Rorvick
P David Sutton
Q Jeff Wendt

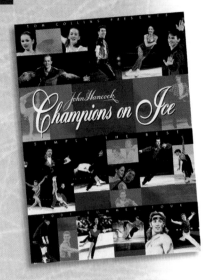

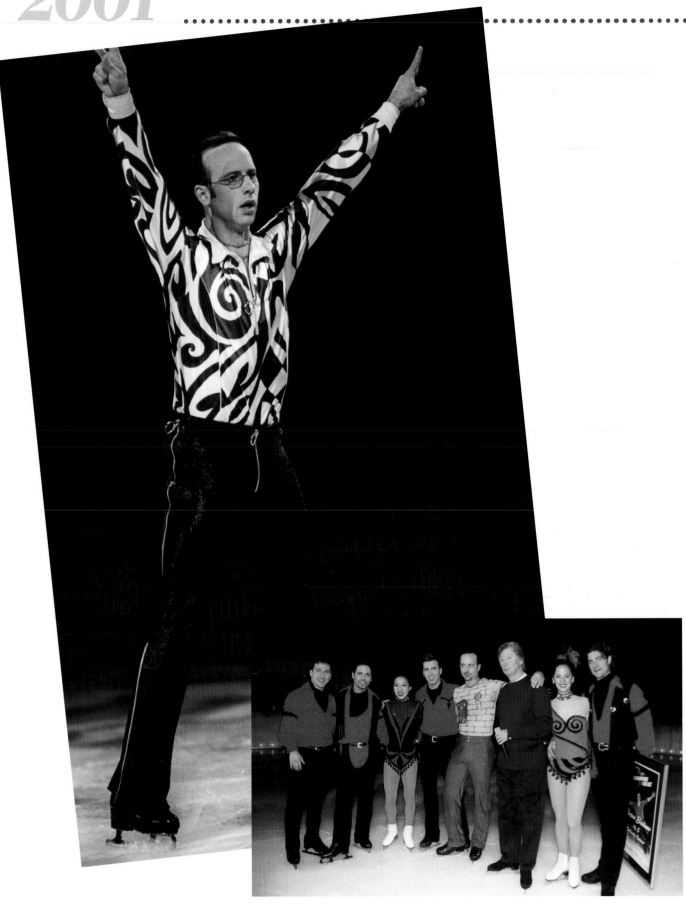

$\mathcal{B}$RIAN BOITANO WAS the focus of the 2001 tour. During the fourth-to-last show, in San Jose, Calif., near Boitano's San Francisco home, Tom Collins and the skaters surprised the tour veteran with an on-ice going-away party. He received his own Champions on Ice rug and wardrobe crate, as well as a Baccarat crystal vase. Michelle Kwan fought back tears as she presented the vase.

"When I was seven years old, I was watching Brian Boitano compete [in the 1988 Winter Olympics]," Kwan said. "I can honestly say that I wouldn't be here if it weren't for you. You've been an inspiration and a role model. Now I want to say you're one of my closest friends, and I will miss you."

"I have a lot of friends in figure skating. My closest friend is Brian Boitano," Tom Collins said into the microphone as he made a rare appearance in skates on the ice. "Brian has mesmerized audiences around the world for over 20 years, and I can assure you it's going to be a long time before we find another male skater with the class, the style and the elegance of Mr. Brian Boitano."

"I consider myself one of the luckiest skaters to have been involved in Champions on Ice for 14 seasons," Boitano said. "And when you think about it, it's a third of my lifetime, not my skating life but my lifetime. Through the years, I've seen a lot of changes, I've met a lot of people coming in and out of shows and met a lot of friends....I cherish the memories and the friendships that I've made....The man that I'll miss the most is Tom Collins. Tommy and I have been through so much together. We've seen the changes in figure skating. We've seen the ups and downs....Tommy is a person who has given me a lot of opportunity, and I will always respect and appreciate that. And Tommy, you're a great producer, but everybody has to know that you're a superb man and an incredible friend."

Boitano took a victory lap to "Thanks for the Memories," then it was back to work. There still was a finale to perform, skated to "The William Tell Overture" in day-glow country fashions.

Boitano had fond memories of the show's opening number as well. The skaters wore black with silver lamé accents, performing to a mix of dance-club music.

Said Collins: "It was harkening back to the old ice shows."

"Tommy's totally old-fashioned," Boitano said. "We were wearing silver lamé in the opening number. It looked like a Holiday on Ice costume, which I loved because I always wanted to be in Holiday on Ice. I told him, 'I finally feel like I'm in Holiday on Ice. It's a lifelong dream come true.'"

2001

Three years removed from their Olympic gold medal, Oksana Kazakova and Artur Dmitriev (left) continued to soar as regulars on tour. Acrobats Vladimir Besedin and Oleksiy Polishchuk (below) take the crowd to new heights with strength, power and humor.

Two Moments

Sᴀʀᴀʜ ʜᴜɢʜᴇs' ʟɪFE CHANGED forever within one hour on the night of Feb. 21, 2002, in Salt Lake City.

After her magnificent Olympic long program, with the crowd still roaring, Hughes didn't immediately step off the ice and go to the "Kiss and Cry" area. Her coach Robin Wagner met her at the boards and turned her around, back toward the ice.

"Close your eyes for a moment," Wagner said to Hughes. "When you open your eyes, I want you to see what you've done. Look at the people standing for you. This is a dream come true."

At the time, Hughes and Wagner had no idea where that performance would put Hughes at evening's end. It could have been fourth place, for all they knew. But that didn't matter.

"As I was watching her look of amazement on the ice," Wagner said, "I realized that this was all going to happen so quickly, and I wanted her to realize as she skated off that it wasn't a dream. I guess it was somewhat selfish in the sense that I didn't want it to end either, so I wanted her to absorb the moment."

"That's one of the best memories that I have," Hughes said. "For Robin to take me and turn me around, there's no way I can thank her enough for that. There's no way to repay that. It's something that I'll definitely remember, probably more than anything else at the Olympics."

Said Wagner: "I think it's something that in the future she should be able to say, 'I'm so glad I just had that moment to look back up at the audience and really see the impact that I made on thousands of people.'"

Hughes was the first of the four top contenders to skate; then the waiting began. She and Wagner sought refuge in the men's locker room, a quiet place during the night of the women's competition. Maria Butyrskaya was the only other skater there.

"I didn't want to watch the monitor," Hughes said. "I changed my clothes. I was in regular clothes and I was just stretching. I remember we were told I definitely had the bronze medal, so I thought, 'Okay, that's really a great accomplishment, very nice.' I put my dress back on, put my skates on. Usually, I take a long time, but I was doing this very, very rapidly. We were sitting there. Irina [Slutskaya] was just finishing up. The cameramen kept wanting to come in and I kept saying, 'I don't want them in, I don't want them in,' because it's a very personal moment. Then, I figured, 'You know what, I have a medal, they can come in,' so Robin let them in."

The final results were coming in at that moment. One of the cameramen, listening on his headset, put up one finger and said, "Hughes first."

"What are you saying?" Wagner asked.

As soon as she said it, coach and pupil were hugging and screaming and falling on the floor.

"Who knew they'd have such startling news?" Hughes said. "I just looked in disbelief because in judged sports, it's so subjective, who knew? The chance of it happening is so slim, it was mind-boggling. At first we weren't sure, then they confirmed it, and we, as you know, fell to the floor. I don't fall when I'm on the ice, but no one said don't fall when you're off the ice."

CAST OF SKATERS

Marina Anissina &
Gwendal Peizerat, FRANCE

1 Vladimir Besedin &
2 Oleksiy Polishchuk, UKRAINE
3 Nicole Bobek, USA
4 Surya Bonaly, FRANCE
5 Shae-Lynn Bourne &
6 Victor Kraatz, CANADA
7 Isabelle Brasseur &
8 Lloyd Eisler, CANADA
9 Philippe Candeloro, FRANCE
10 Sasha Cohen, USA
11 Rudy Galindo, USA
12 Timothy Goebel, USA
13 Irina Grigorian, RUSSIA
14 Dan Hollander, USA
15 Sarah Hughes, USA

16 Oksana Kazakova &
17 Artur Dmitriev, RUSSIA
18 Michelle Kwan, USA
19 Naomi Lang &
20 Peter Tchernyshev, USA
21 Viktor Petrenko, UKRAINE
22 Evgeni Plushenko, RUSSIA
23 Elizabeth Punsalan &
24 Jerod Swallow, USA
25 Irina Slutskaya, RUSSIA
26 Elvis Stojko, CANADA
27 Michael Weiss, USA
   Alexei Yagudin, RUSSIA

ALSO...

A Tom Collins
B Brian Klavano
C Sarah Kawahara

THE STORY OF THE 2002 tour was its amazing length and the confusion that it would invariably cause from day to day.

"Normally, if it's 20 cities, I have no problem knowing where I am and where I've been," said tour veteran Michael Weiss. "But 93 shows? In 85 different cities? If you remember all that stuff, you're a genius. I couldn't keep up with it. We changed so many hotels that a lot of times I'd check out and wouldn't turn in the room key, which was just a plastic card. So, say, I'd be coming in at 1:00 A.M. or 2:00 A.M. after a bus ride back from some venue, and I'd go to room 726 and pull out my key and try to get in and it's not working. That's because I was in 726 in the last hotel. In this hotel, I'm in 1412. I did that three or four times on this tour, gotten off on the wrong floor and gone to the room number of the hotel I was in before."

And when the tour was over, there was the adjustment of slowly returning to normalcy.

"You get used to living out of a suitcase," said Jerod Swallow, "and, believe it or not, when you go home, you have to adjust to not living out of the suitcase. We were in the suitcase still for another 48 hours when we got home."

"If it's not in your suitcase," said his wife Liz Punsalan, "you don't know where it is. You're totally lost."

Sarah Hughes, the new Olympic champion, went to high school Monday through Thursday during the spring, then joined the tour Friday, Saturday and Sunday. She still skated in 38 shows. Most years, that would be the entire tour, or close to it. This year, it wasn't even half the dates.

"It was such a great thrill to go out and skate after they'd say 'Olympic Champion Sarah Hughes' because I know what went into that title, and it was a lot of work and it didn't happen by accident," Hughes said. "It was a lot of preparation, it was a lot of work, it was a lot of thought, a lot of direction, a lot of time — and a lot of luck. I'd think about it for a second before I started my program every night."

Tom Collins gave her the position of honor when she was on tour — closing the show with the final individual number.

"She reminds me at an early stage of Peggy Fleming, with those long legs of hers," Collins said. "She has that grace now. She's going to do very, very well in the skating world."

The September 11 terrorist attacks had an impact on the 2002 tour. Collins invited Joanna Glick, sister of United flight 93 hero Jeremy Glick, to skate in a few shows near her home in New Jersey.

And now, onto 2003, the 25th year of Champions on Ice. The tour will once again be split in two: there will be 23 shows in December 2002 and January 2003 on the winter tour, followed by 39 on the summer tour, running from April to June. Headliners will include tour veterans Michelle Kwan, Sarah Hughes and Timothy Goebel, among others. Up-and-coming stars will pop up here and there near their hometowns, as always. In short, it will be very much like any other year on tour, now 25 and counting.

One photo; tons of talent: Top-four finishers at the 2002 Olympics in Salt Lake City pose for a rare portrait at the start of the tour in Orlando.

Timothy Goebel (left) represents the tour's new generation, while Oksana Kazakova and Artur Dmitriev (below) carry on the legend of Russian pairs skating.

Red, white and blue: the tour's star-spangled finale included Naomi Lang and Peter Tchernyshev (top) and Evgeni Plushenko (right).

A Day in the Life...
April 12, 2002

The show in Baltimore was over, the next tour stop in Washington, D.C., was scheduled to begin in 19½ hours.

*T*HIS WAS NOT the most difficult trip on the tour, this drive down I-95 from Baltimore to Washington. Just two days earlier, the skaters had started the day in Atlanta, flown to Norfolk, Va., performed in Hampton, Va., and bused to Washington, D.C. That's two states and the District of Columbia, all in a day's work.

On this night, the skaters hopped on two tour buses to make the one-hour trip from Baltimore Arena to the Four Seasons Hotel in Washington. But they left behind a small army of men and women who had some heavy lifting to do. Their job was to move 273,500 pounds of equipment out of Baltimore Arena, pack it into five trucks, then travel to Washington and move it into the MCI Center early that morning. It was the equivalent of moving 23 families of four out of one house and into another — within 12 hours.

This was how April 12, 2002 began for the skaters, staff and crew of Champions on Ice. In the 24 hours that would make up this day on the tour, there would be a visit by one skater to the White House, an appearance by another on NBC's *Today Show*, a pick-up hockey game, sightseeing, shopping, eating — and a fair amount of skating.

In some ways, it was a typical day on tour. In others, it was the most unusual day of all.

In the whirlwind of the Champions on Ice tour, 19½ hours was plenty of time to get ready for the next show. Plenty of time to rest, to play, to practice and to prepare as the clock started ticking off the seconds of Friday, April 12, 2002.

12:00 midnight

*T*WO AND A HALF hours after a crowd of 11,000 left Baltimore Arena, four Champions on Ice stage hands push a large blue case loaded with spotlights up a ramp into the last of the tour's five semi trucks. The tour's "load-out" is almost complete.

12:01 a.m.

In Washington, the skaters have been checked into the Four Seasons Hotel in Georgetown for about an hour. In her room, Sasha Cohen begins a homework assignment: reading Dr. Zhivago.

Husband-and-wife ice dancers Jerod Swallow and Liz Punsalan switch between CNN and ESPN in their room before falling asleep.

12:08 a.m.

*I*N A STRETCH LIMO on her way to New York City for an 8:50 a.m. appearance on the *Today Show*, Irina Slutskaya talks on her cell phone to her husband in Moscow, where it's early in the morning. The limo driver hits the brakes. Slutskaya slides off the smooth leather seats and lands on the limo floor at the feet of tour publicist Lynn Plage, who is accompanying Slutskaya to New York. The Olympic silver medalist giggles in a heap on the floor.

12:10 a.m.

The final lighting case is loaded onto the final truck in the dark, lonely parking lot of Baltimore Arena. The arena is empty. Thirty-nine local workers walk to their cars to head home. Ten permanent members of the tour's crew head to their bus for the ride to Washington.

12:15 a.m

BACK AT THE FOUR Seasons Hotel, Sarah Hughes already is asleep as her mother Amy turns out the lights in their room. They flew to Washington from their home in New York earlier in the evening and checked into the hotel. Sarah has laryngitis, so she wrote notes to her mother all evening. They ordered room service and turned on the television and were surprised to see a replay of the exhibition from the recent World Figure Skating Championships in Nagano, which Sarah did not attend. As they ate dinner and watched skating, Sarah grabbed a pen and scribbled a message to her mother: "Could this be any better?"

12:20 a.m.

A room service waiter arrives at Michelle Kwan's door, carrying the caesar salad she ordered. Michelle watches *Oceans 11* on the hotel's movie channel before going to sleep.

12:25 a.m.

Irina Slutskaya and Lynn Plage stop along the New Jersey Turnpike to buy two essential items: M&M's and *Seventeen* magazine. Irina picks *Seventeen* because she wants to use the magazine to help her get better at reading and understanding English. She opens the magazine inside the limo, with Lynn by her side to help her with words she doesn't know.

12:30 a.m.

In the lobby of the Four Seasons Hotel, tour founder and executive producer Tom Collins meets with his son Michael, the tour manager, to discuss the show in Baltimore.

Sasha Cohen puts down her book and turns out the lights in the room she is sharing with her mother, Galina.

1:00 a.m.

TIM GOEBEL HOPS into the shower in his room after eating a late snack in the lobby bar, then goes to sleep.

1:02 a.m.

Back in Baltimore, five shiny black tour trucks and the crew bus pull out of the Baltimore Arena parking lot for the drive down I-95 to Washington's MCI Center.

1:15 a.m.

From her room at the Four Seasons, Irina Grigorian, the tour's hula-hoop act, calls her mother and husband in Las Vegas. She rooms with Irina Slutskaya on the road, so she has the room all to herself tonight and can stay up as late as she wants without bothering anyone.

1:30 a.m.

At Michael Weiss' home in McLean, Va., Elvis Stojko, Dan Hollander, Peter Tchernyshev and their host eat ice cream and jump on the Weiss family trampoline, not necessarily in that order. Michael and his wife Lisa drove their house guests home from Baltimore Arena; because the tour is staying in Washington for several days, it's a rare opportunity for the skaters to get away from a hotel for a night.

1:40 a.m.

Isabelle Brasseur and her husband Rocky Marval, a former pairs skater turned agent who once toured with Champions on Ice, go to sleep in their room at the Four Seasons. Their 18-month-old daughter Gabriella has been asleep for more than an hour.

1:55 a.m.

THE FIVE TRUCKS and one bus arrive at the MCI Center in downtown Washington. Two of the trucks drive down a steep ramp into the loading dock inside the arena, including the rig that holds all the exercise equipment and backstage games for the skaters. Three others must park on the street overnight, including the wardrobe truck. There is no room for them inside the arena because pieces of the Washington Wizards' basketball floor, pulled up to make room for the ice for the tour's show, are in the way.

2:00 a.m.

$\mathscr{P}$UTTING ASIDE his files and paperwork, Tom Collins turns off the lights in his suite at the Four Seasons and goes to sleep.

2:10 a.m.

Irina Slutskaya and Lynn Plage check into the Essex House in New York City.

2:15 a.m.

Philippe Candeloro and three friends from Air France visit a Georgetown nightclub. On the dance floor, "women like to join me," Candeloro says with a smile.

2:20 a.m.

Irina Slutskaya jumps into the shower in her hotel room. There's no hot water. She washes her face quickly and jumps right back out of the shower. Within 10 minutes, Slutskaya is asleep.

2:35 a.m.

$\mathscr{M}$ICHAEL WEISS says good night to the guests scattered throughout his home. Elvis Stojko is sleeping in the guest room; Dan Hollander is in Michael's son Christopher's room, and Peter Tchernyshev takes the sofa in the family room.

3:00 a.m.

$\mathscr{P}$HILIPPE CANDELORO returns to the hotel, turns on the TV in his room, sits on his bed and falls fast asleep.

4:30 a.m.

Staff members of Hightopps Catering out of Baltimore arrive at MCI Center and begin setting up the room – known appropriately enough as Catering – that will serve as a dining room throughout the day. This room is located deep inside the arena, near the trucks that have driven inside the building. Breakfast, lunch and dinner will be served for the crew; dinner and snacks for the skaters and staff. Before arriving at the arena, the caterers made a special stop to buy four dozen donuts for the local stage hands who will unload the trucks in a few hours.

5:20 a.m.

The alarm goes off in Irina Slutskaya's room at the Essex House in New York, but this is not the time she is supposed to awaken. The alarm must have been set by the previous guest. She shakes her head, hits the clock and the alarm shuts off.

6:00 a.m.

*T*HE ALARM GOES off again in Slutskaya's room. This still isn't the time she is supposed to get up. She hits the clock again. The alarm shuts off. Again.

6:10 a.m.

On the crew bus, the tour's lighting director and jack-of-all-trades can't sleep. So Dean Moyé gets up and begins his work day by locating the phone lines in all the production offices backstage at the MCI Center, lines the staff will use when they arrive hours later. He checks the phone lines to make sure they are working. He dials his cell phone. The reception is bad. This is the kind of information the staff, skaters and their agents don't want to hear, but it's Moyé's job to let them know.

6:30 a.m.

*S*ARAH HUGHES AWAKENS in her room at the Four Seasons. Her mother Amy has been tossing and turning for some time. Her mind is racing. In less than an hour, they are going to the White House to meet President Bush. "What if my kid can't talk," Amy Hughes is asking herself, "on this of all days."

Jim Means, the driver of the truck carrying the tour's wardrobe, among other items, awakens on Sixth St. NW in Washington. His was one of the trucks that was stuck on the street overnight.

6:31 a.m.

Sarah Hughes speaks. Amy Hughes smiles. Her daughter's laryngitis is gone. Once again, Sarah Hughes' timing is perfect.

6:40 a.m.

Back in New York City, the alarm goes off again in Irina Slutskaya's room. This still isn't the time she is supposed to awaken. She hits the clock. Again. The alarm shuts off. Again.

6:45 a.m.

Tour production manager Paul Hendrickson awakens in his bunk in the crew bus deep inside the MCI Center. He looks out the window of the bus and sees nothing but concrete and cinder block. Another arena, he says to himself. It often takes him a moment to remember which one it is. Sometimes he and his crew will go three or four days without seeing the sun. This is one of those mornings.

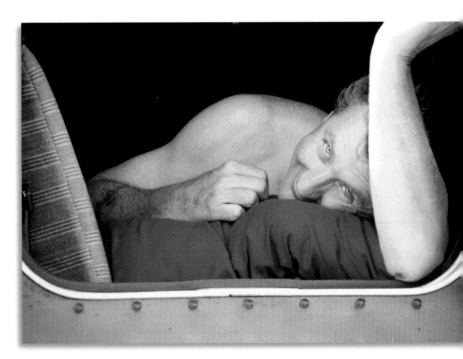

6:55 a.m.

Mike Reed, the driver of the truck carrying all the backstage games, the pool and ping pong tables and the exercise equipment for the skaters, awakens to the sound of his windup Baby Ben alarm clock ringing beside his bunk inside his truck in the MCI Center. He, too, wakes up to the sight of concrete.

7:00 a.m.

PAUL HENDRICKSON steps out of the crew bus and begins his day by meeting with a building official who is there to greet him. He is fighting a nasty cold, and he is not the only person on the tour who is. Several members of his crew are also sick. It got so bad last night in Baltimore that he drank half a bottle of Nyquil before conking out on the crew bus on the way to Washington. A doctor has been called to treat the crew this afternoon before their germs knock out most of the tour, skaters included.

7:05 a.m.

Jim Means drives the wardrobe truck off the street and into the loading dock.

7:20 a.m.

Sarah Hughes, Amy Hughes and coach Robin Wagner get into a cab at the Four Seasons. They're heading 12 blocks away, to the White House.

7:15 a.m.

In New York City, the phone rings in Irina Slutskaya's room at the Essex House. This, finally, is the time she is supposed to get up. "Where am I?" Slutskaya says into the phone. Laughing at herself, she jumps into the shower. The hot water is working now. Finally, something has gone right in Slutskaya's morning.

In Washington, D.C., the phone rings in Isabelle Brasseur's room at the Four Seasons. This is the wake-up call for Isabelle and her husband Rocky. Little Gabriella is still sleeping, "for once," Isabelle laughs.

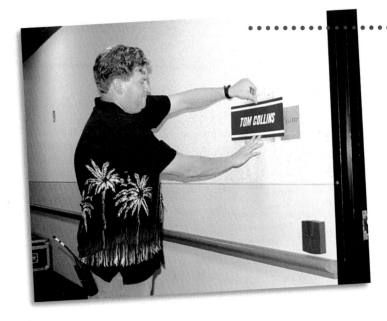

7:29 a.m.

The MCI Center is quickly coming to life. Jeff Wendt, the tour's backstage coordinator, charges through the backstage hallways taping blue signs beside the doors to the offices that tour officials and staff will use for the shows today and tomorrow in Washington. "TOM COLLINS," reads one sign. "PAUL HENDRICKSON," reads another. This way, the crew knows where to take the cases that belong to staff members when they come off the trucks. Included in the items that travel is a full office for Tom Collins: a sofa, love seat, chair, ottoman, coffee table, three end tables and three lamps.

7:30 a.m.

Sarah Hughes, her mother and her coach enter the White House grounds at the Northwest guard gate on Pennsylvania Avenue. They are met by Jim Wilkinson, special assistant to the President.

Irina Slutskaya meets Lynn Plage in the lobby of the Essex House in New York. They check out.

7:50 a.m.

MICHAEL WEISS gets up at home in McLean, Va. As he wanders downstairs, he sees his three-year-old daughter, Annie Mae, standing by the sofa, looking at Peter Tchernyshev. She's waking Peter by moving her index finger up and down across his lips while making noises with her lips: "Bbbbb-bbbb-bbbbb."

8:00 a.m.

SARAH HUGHES, ACCOMPANIED by her mother and coach, eats Frosted Flakes for breakfast in the White House mess with several advisors to the President, including Karen Hughes, who at the time was one of Bush's top assistants. Karen Hughes has been joking with friends for weeks that she and Sarah are related. Karen gives Sarah a photo that shows Karen holding a front-page "Hughes Soars" headline that appeared the day after Sarah won her Olympic gold medal.

8:01 a.m.

IRINA SLUTSKAYA arrives at the Today Show. She eats a bagel with cream cheese and heads to makeup.

8:02 a.m.

A hotel van pulls away from the Four Seasons carrying tour manager Michael Collins and his brother Marty, the tour coordinator, along with Lloyd Eisler, Isabelle Brasseur and Rocky Marval. They are going to the Fairfax Ice Arena in the Washington suburbs, the rink where Michael Weiss trains, to play pick-up hockey. Isabelle, who is studying photography, has brought her camera to record the event. She also has brought the tiniest fan, little Gabriella.

8:03 a.m.

The first blue case comes off the first truck inside the MCI Center. It's a box filled with equipment for the tour's elaborate sound system. It is pushed on its wheels through a hallway, down one of the entryways and onto the ice. This is the beginning of the process that will turn a basketball and hockey venue into the ice-cold stage for a figure skating show in a matter of a few hours.

8:07 a.m.

"That one goes at center ice," Paul Hendrickson shouts to a local stage hand pushing another blue case on wheels. "At the red line is fine."

8:15 a.m.

*I*RINA SLUTSKAYA practices on the ice rink at Rockefeller Center not even 12 hours after she left the ice in Baltimore. She's in full costume preparing for her cowgirl tour number, "Cotton-eyed Joe." She's not only talking on the *Today Show*, she's skating.

8:20 a.m.

Back at the MCI Center, wardrobe supervisor Roger Bathurst helps workers maneuver the tour's traveling washing machine into a bathroom beside his backstage office. He screws off the shower head in the bathroom shower and screws on a faucet that allows him to hook up the hose to the washing machine.

8:27 a.m.

Michael Weiss and Friends (minus Dan Hollander, who decides to skip the hockey game and sleep in) pile into Michael's Durango for the drive to the Fairfax Ice Arena. Michael picks up his cell phone a few minutes into the ride to call an FM radio station in Washington, DC-101, for an interview about that night's show. Interviews such as this are part of the skaters' job to promote the tour.

8:30 a.m.

At the Four Seasons, ice dancer Shae-Lynn Bourne gets up and decides she is going to work out. Her usual routine is to work out in the morning or the evening at the hotel; there's not enough time for her to exercise backstage at the arena after she and Victor Kraatz skate in the second act of the show.

8:34 a.m.

Back at the MCI Center, the last of 25 speakers, 34 motor boxes and 24 blue production cases, among other items, comes off the first truck, the one carrying all the sound equipment.

8:35 a.m.

Michelle Kwan opens her hotel room door at the Four Seasons and picks up her *USA Today* from the hallway floor.

8:36 a.m.

SHAE-LYNN BOURNE walks into the health club at the Four Seasons.

8:37 a.m.

SHAE-LYNN BOURNE walks out of the health club at the Four Seasons. Not motivated to work out — and feeling hungry — she heads to the restaurant, orders scrambled eggs and coffee and starts making calls on her cell phone.

8:50 a.m.

On the *Today Show*, Katie Couric interviews Irina Slutskaya for three minutes on the ice, then asks Irina to perform her tour number. Slutskaya is ready, except for one thing. She realizes she is wearing her watch. Not wanting to be bothered by it as she skates, she takes it off and asks Couric to hold it. Katie obliges.

8:56 a.m.

At the MCI Center, the first piece of the tour's 20,000-pound sound system goes into the air. It's the amp rack, hoisted to the ceiling by two one-ton chain motors to take its place high above center ice, where the MCI Center's scoreboard sits. It won't come down for 31 hours, until after the tour's second and last show in Washington.

9:00 a.m.

AT THE WHITE HOUSE, Sarah Hughes moves from one meeting with presidential advisors to another, listening to briefings about how women and children are being treated in Afghanistan. Sarah met Vice President Dick Cheney at the men's Olympic gold medal hockey game in Salt Lake City in February, and the new women's Olympic figure skating gold medalist asked if there was something she could do to help with the situation in Afghanistan. The Vice President recommended her for a mission to that war-torn nation to support women and girls as they assimilate back into society, including going back to school. The mission was canceled, but Sarah's interest remains.

9:01 a.m.

BACK AT THE MCI Center, the last crate comes off the second truck, the lighting truck. That truck sits beside the first truck, unloaded and empty.

Tour executive producer Tom Collins awakens at the Four Seasons and immediately turns on his cell phone to begin his work day.

9:02 a.m.

An unlikely group of hockey players takes the ice in Fairfax, Va. They can skate; there's no doubt about that. But can they play hockey? Joined by other pick-up hockey players who've shown up just by chance, including a few women, Michael Weiss' gang begins playing. Lloyd Eisler is voted the man most likely to be mistaken for a hockey player; he has a black eye after being hit — unintentionally — by Isabelle Brasseur during their triple twist in the Baltimore show last night. Peter Tchernyshev is voted least likely to be mistaken for a hockey player. He is playing in his figure skates.

9:07 a.m.

Tour media coordinator Grant Rorvick turns on his cell phone after waking up in the Four Seasons. There are 14 new messages since he went to sleep at 2:20 a.m. They're all from reporters or other members of the media, requesting interviews with skaters or access to a particular tour stop.

9:15 a.m.

Roger Bathurst throws a load of clothes into his washing machine at the MCI Center. Included in this pile: Rudy Galindo's "In the Navy" shirt.

9:27 a.m.

O**N THE ICE,** Paul Hendrickson opens a long blue box holding the four U.S. flags that unfurl from the rafters during the show's patriotic finale. The flags in their black containers won't be attached to the sound system and hoisted to the ceiling for another couple of hours. At the moment, workers are linking the 24 speakers that are clustered together to form the sound system. The flags will be attached once the sound system is ready. They are in one of about 50 cases that litter the ice at the moment.

9:40 a.m.

Stage hands set up the exercise equipment backstage. They position the treadmill, two elliptical trainers, two StairMasters, two stationary bikes and four PlayStations. "All the stuff that keeps the kids from going crazy," says driver Mike Reed, who is entrusted with the equipment from city to city.

10:03 a.m.

"Do the pool table now," backstage coordinator Jeff Wendt tells six workers in the arena. What's an ice show without a pool table? Off comes the top of a big blue box and the tour's pool table is revealed. It is nestled beside rows and rows of stacked chairs backstage.

10:00 a.m.

A**T THE FOUR SEASONS,** tour founder Tom Collins and tour star Michelle Kwan bump into one another in the health club. Michelle is already on the treadmill; Tom hops on an exercise bike.

Liz Punsalan and Jerod Swallow awaken. Liz makes coffee in the room; Jerod fires up their computer to check e-mail. While on-line, they balance their checkbook and order a bicycle case for Jerod, who plans to bring his bike on the next leg of the tour.

Philippe Candeloro gets up in his room and goes downstairs for coffee.

10:15 a.m.

Room service arrives at Tim Goebel's room. His bill was $28 for eggs, bacon and a large pot of coffee. The coffee by itself cost a staggering $17. "But it was worth it," he says later.

10:30 a.m.

Sarah Hughes walks into the Oval Office and shakes the hand of the President of the United States. "So you're the one who does all those triple jumps?" George W. Bush asks kindly, and Sarah says yes, she's the one. Sarah introduces her mother and coach to the President, explaining later she did so "because they were a little nervous." Bush shows them around his office, explaining the design of the rug on the floor, talking about the history of his desk and discussing several paintings. They speak of his concerns about Afghanistan and Sarah's interest in the subject. The President gives Sarah several fatherly tips: "Go to college," he says. "Save your money," is another. Says Bush, "I don't want to see you driving a Rolls Royce." Sarah smiles, and says hours later, "He gave me some good advice." They talk about whether she'd be in another Olympics, and she says it's "possible." Robin Wagner says she was more nervous during this meeting than she was during the women's long program at the Olympics. And Amy Hughes? She starts telling the President about what an incredible few months it has been, with her daughter winning the gold medal, and now this, and then she blurts out, "I can't believe all this. I need to pinch myself to make sure it's true." The President replies, "I'll pinch you," and he reaches over to give her a playful little pinch on the arm.

10:31 a.m.

Irina Slutskaya and Lynn Plage board the Delta Shuttle at LaGuardia for the flight to Washington's Reagan National Airport. At security, all of Slutskaya's luggage is searched. This isn't unique treatment; many passengers traveling to Washington National go through special security checks since the September 11 terrorist attacks.

10:40 a.m.

Backstage man Jeff Wendt moves the hands on a big clock he has set on top of the PlayStation facing the exercise equipment. This is the area that draws more skaters during the evening than any other spot, and they'll need this clock to gauge their schedules as they stretch on the mats, use the workout equipment and play with the video games.

10:45 a.m.

Sarah Hughes and Co. say their goodbyes to President Bush and move on to another meeting, this one with noted former figure skater and current national security adviser Condoleezza Rice. They've met before, Rice and Hughes, and as they are chatting in Rice's office, her phone rings. As Rice listens intently to the person on the other end, her visitors fidget nervously. "Should we be sitting here?" Sarah, her mother and Robin Wagner mouth to one another. They stay, and Rice soon is off the phone.

11:00 a.m.

*A*FTER SPENDING one-and-a-half hours on the ice in Fairfax playing hockey, the skaters travel to Michael Weiss' home for sandwiches and sushi. Lisa Weiss arrives with Sasha Cohen and her mother, Galina, whom she picked up at the Four Seasons. The Weiss family trampoline comes out of the garage and onto the driveway and everyone takes his or her turn. Michael's father, Greg, a member of the 1964 U.S. Olympic team as a gymnast, helps Elvis Stojko and Sasha work on their back flips.

Jerod Swallow finds a post office near the hotel and mails several packages home. Skaters are always trying to lighten their load as the tour moves on, sending items home along the way.

11:15 a.m.

Michelle Kwan leaves the health club and goes to her room to take a shower and get ready for the day.

11:30 a.m.

Fighting a bad cold and sleeping in as long as she can, Naomi Lang, Shae-Lynn Bourne's roommate on the road, awakens.

Viktor Petrenko wakes up in his room at the Four Seasons. He had been thinking of playing hockey but slept right through it.

Liz Punsalan and Jerod Swallow walk into Twist, a Georgetown bistro. Liz orders a mixed-greens salad and Jerod chooses the peasant veggie soup.

11:25 a.m.

*L*OU McCLARY, tour security director, calls Dean Moyé, tour lighting director, to discuss the tour's stalker file. They travel with a three-ring binder listing the names of all known stalkers who might want to show up at a particular tour stop. They treat this very seriously and will alert building officials of the names later in the day.

11:44 a.m.

At the MCI Center, a crew member places the containers holding all four U.S. flags onto hooks attached to the bottom of the 20,000-pound sound system.

11:57 a.m.

During a routine check, Paul Hendrickson notices that one of the four U.S. flags has been attached backwards to the sound system. He and another worker take the huge flag in its black wrapping off the hooks and flip it around, then reattach it. "This is one place where if you have the flag hanging the wrong way, people would notice," Hendrickson says of Washington.

11:50 a.m.

Shae-Lynn Bourne ventures out into Georgetown in search of CDs. This will be her off-ice workout for the day.

12:00 noon

MICHELLE KWAN walks past Twist in Georgetown. Spotting Liz Punsalan and Jerod Swallow, she goes inside and joins them.

12:05 p.m.

After landing at National Airport, Irina Slutskaya notices a man staring at her. "Good job," he says to her. She smiles, thanks him and keeps walking. "They likes me," Slutskaya whispers to publicist Lynn Plage.

12:15 p.m.

Still in his room, Tim Goebel repacks his luggage, trying to keep one step ahead in the packing marathon known as tour life. He still has another day in Washington before the tour hits the road again. He also takes time to call his mother at their home-away-from-home in Los Angeles to check in and say hello.

12:27 p.m.

At the MCI Center, the sound system, draped in black, begins to rise off the ice toward the ceiling, lifted by a dozen thick wires. The show's lighting trusses, which hold the spotlights that will create the myriad colors and designs during the skaters' numbers, also slowly begin to rise off the ice toward the rafters. Attached to the trusses are wires holding several dozen tiny bags, an inch in diameter, each with a mixture of oxidizer, aluminum powder and titanium. These will become the show's fireworks display.

12:50 p.m.

Back at the Four Seasons, Irina Slutskaya takes a nap. Her roommate, Irina Grigorian, reads a book on Microsoft Windows XP.

1:00 p.m. ....

LIZ PUNSALAN and Jerod Swallow invite the tour's athletic trainer, Eric Lang, to join them on their trip to the National Building Museum to see several exhibits, including the new World Trade Center design proposals.

Viktor Petrenko, Oksana Kazakova and Philippe Candeloro's attorney Sergio Canovas eat sushi in Georgetown. Candeloro joins his friends from Air France at La Madeleine, where he orders a soufflé.

Tim Goebel gets on the phone again, this time for 15 minutes to talk to a reporter from Cleveland Scene, an Ohio entertainment publication, to help promote the upcoming tour stop in the town where he once trained.

1:15 p.m.

AFTER BEING INTERVIEWED by Voice of America on the topics of Afghan children as well as the Olympics, and watching Ari Fleischer's briefing with reporters in the White House press room, Sarah Hughes leaves the White House. As soon as she and her mother and coach get into a cab for the short ride back to the Four Seasons, her cell phone rings. It's her brother Matt, calling from college. "How was it?" he asks. "The President pinched Mom!" Sarah screams into the phone.

1:20 p.m.

The hotel van leaves Michael Weiss' home to return the hockey players, Isabelle Brasseur, Sasha Cohen and family members to the Four Seasons. Elvis Stojko, Dan Hollander and Peter Tchernyshev stay behind with Michael. While eating chocolate chip cookie dough ice cream, they watch a movie on Lifetime about an anorexic gymnast.

1:30 p.m.

Shae-Lynn Bourne finishes her CD shopping in Georgetown. She ends up buying 20 CDs that she hopes will yield a few songs for future programs.

1:35 p.m.

Tom Collins meets with tour performance director Brian Klavano to go over Tom's notes on the last few shows. They are constantly tinkering with their daily product; on this day, still early in the tour, they are discussing the tour's running order to make sure they like who follows whom onto the ice. They also check the timing of the flags and fireworks in the finale.

1:50 p.m.

*I*SABELLE BRASSEUR tries to take a nap with Gabriella in their room while husband Rocky finds a photo shop in Georgetown that will develop her film before they leave for the show in less than two hours.

1:58 p.m.

Rudy Galindo shows up at Nicole Bobek's room to watch the upcoming *Maury Povich Show*. The show's topic: "Are you really the father?" They sit on the bed, enraptured and giggling.

2:00 p.m.

*A*T THE MCI CENTER, the ice has been cleared of all the cases, and the arena is now ready for a skating show. Their work complete, some crew members walk four blocks to their hotel, the Grand Hyatt, to check in, take a shower and take a nap. Because there are two shows in Washington — one tonight and a matinee tomorrow — the crew will enjoy a rare night in a hotel and a rare evening off from having to dismantle the show and send it packing to another city.

2:15 p.m.

Sasha Cohen, one of several skaters fighting a cold, takes a nap in her room. Meanwhile, Tim Goebel hops into a cab to go to the MCI Center for extra practice time. He wants to work especially on his quadruple jumps and spins.

2:25 p.m.

*G*etting ready for their day at the office, roommates Shae-Lynn Bourne and Naomi Lang turn on the television in their room to catch the end of *One Life to Live*. When that ends, they watch five minutes of *General Hospital* before flicking off the TV. "If you haven't watched a soap in weeks," they tell each other, laughing, "you're totally caught up after watching for five minutes."

2:30 p.m.

Isabelle Brasseur gives up on trying to take a nap. Gabriella is more interested in running around the room.

2:35 p.m.

Viktor Petrenko walks into Georgetown Mall and buys a DVD of the movie *Airplane*. "I love comedies," he says, "and I love this movie."

2:45 p.m.

Sarah Hughes and Robin Wagner take a cab for the 22-block trip from the Four Seasons to the MCI Center.

3:00 p.m.

$\mathcal{M}$ICHELLE KWAN STOPS in at Dean & DeLuca for a chicken Caesar salad.

Evgeni Plushenko, who went to sleep not long after midnight, finally awakens in his room. He slept for nearly 15 hours. "I was very tired," he explains.

$\mathcal{L}$IZ PUNSALAN, JEROD Swallow and athletic trainer Eric Lang return to the hotel from the National Building Museum. Although they didn't have as much time as they would have liked to study the exhibits, they found themselves reminiscing on the way back to the Four Seasons about a similar trip seven years ago in Washington when the three of them were joined by Brian Boitano and Jill Trenary for a day of museum hopping and sightseeing. For tour veterans like Liz, Jerod and Eric, this is becoming a tradition: "Not just the sightseeing," Eric says, "but the reminiscing." When they get out of the car at the Four Seasons, they immediately step back into the reality of tour life: they bump into Rudy Galindo and Nicole Bobek, who are carrying their laundry. Liz gives Rudy an extra Eva Cassidy CD she had with her, knowing Rudy did not yet have it.

3:02 p.m.

Dealing with a six-hour time difference between the eastern United States and France, Philippe Candeloro calls home to Paris to say good night to his wife and small daughter. Tired from being out so late last night, he then takes a nap.

3:05 p.m.

Liz Punsalan and Jerod Swallow head to their new haunt, Twist, for coffee. This time, they are joined by tour coordinator Marty Collins and media coordinator Grant Rorvick.

3:10 p.m.

Michael Weiss and friends hop into his car for the ride from McLean, Va., to the MCI Center to begin their work day. On the way, they pick up Michael's mother, Margie, and his daughter, Annie Mae, for whom Margie has been babysitting at her home.

3:12 p.m.

*T*HE TOUR BUS sits on Pennsylvania Avenue near the Four Seasons Hotel, waiting to take the skaters who are still in the hotel to the MCI Center for tonight's show. Eric Lang hauls 80 pounds of physical therapy and medical equipment to the bus, then, with some time to kill, makes a coffee run. As he explains: "It's a time for all of us Type A's to hang out, pace for a spell and take bets on who will be late for the bus today."

3:35 p.m.

Sarah Hughes joins Tim Goebel on the ice at the MCI Center for an extra practice session with her coach, Robin Wagner. Another one of those tour members who are fighting colds, Sarah hasn't practiced in the past three days.

3:38 p.m.

Several dogs appear at the MCI Center — with security agents in tow. These aren't pets; they're bomb-sniffing dogs performing a sweep of the building.

3:40 p.m.

Michelle Kwan steps onto the bus, puts her bag on a seat and then dashes to the CVS drug store she spots across the street to run an errand.

3:45 p.m.

*T*om Collins stands on the corner watching his world go by. He's on the sidewalk along Pennsylvania Avenue chatting with son Michael as the skaters make their way to the bus. The bus left Tom behind — for a few minutes, anyway — in Orlando a week earlier. That's not going to happen this time or, most likely, ever again.

3:47 p.m.

Michelle Kwan returns to the bus. On the sidewalk, three college-aged women in sweatshirts turn to look as a fan stops Michelle for an autograph. One of the women recognizes Kwan and starts jumping up and down, hitting her friends on the shoulder. Michelle signs autographs for three men in business suits, then gets onto the bus. The women never ask for an autograph; they just stand and watch as Michelle signs for others.

3:50 p.m.

The bus pulls away from the curb and begins to zigzag through Washington traffic to the MCI Center.

3:52 p.m.

Shae-Lynn Bourne is wearing her headphones on the bus, listening to one of her new CDs. She writes ideas about the songs on Post-it Notes that she attaches to the CD. "There are usually one or two good songs on each CD," she says.

3:55 p.m.

The bus passes the White House. A few skaters turn to look.

4:00 p.m.

AT THE MCI CENTER, a doctor arrives to see members of the crew. This is not a normal occurrence. Many members of the crew are sick, including production manager Paul Hendrickson. A local doctor was called in immediately because if the bug isn't treated promptly, it will spread like wildfire to the skaters and staff, some of whom already are sick. By the time all the patients are seen in the production office backstage, the doctor has written numerous prescriptions and a nearby pharmacy is about to enjoy an unexpected windfall.

4:10 p.m.

The skaters' bus arrives at the MCI Center, pulls into the loading dock, drives down the ramp and glides to a stop inside the building. To reach their dressing rooms, the skaters have a two-minute walk past the five empty tour trucks, rows and rows of empty blue cases and the exercise equipment.

4:15 p.m.

Already finished practicing, Tim Goebel walks to Catering to eat an early dinner. He fixes himself a salad and picks at assorted crackers, fruit and munchies.

4:20 p.m.

Isabelle Brasseur's pictures from the morning hockey game are a huge hit in the backstage hallway near the dressing rooms. Michael Weiss sifts through them. Soon, Elvis Stojko comes along and asks to see the photos. Peter Tchernyshev also comes by; he's still hearing from his friends about his unorthodox decision to wear his figure skates.

4:30 p.m.

Sasha Cohen stays in her hotel room as long as possible, eating chicken soup and drinking orange juice to fight her cold before catching a cab with her mother to the arena.

4:40 p.m.

At the MCI Center, Jerod Swallow sets up his skate sharpening machine backstage and sees two customers, fellow ice dancers Naomi Lang and Liz Punsalan.

4:45 p.m.

Irina Slutskaya wakes up for the fifth time today. She calls her mother and her husband in Moscow and gets ready to take another limo — this one from the Four Seasons to the MCI Center for tonight's show. She was given permission to miss the bus because of her hectic schedule promoting the tour on TV this morning.

5:00 p.m.

SARAH HUGHES LEAVES the ice. She was not the only skater who practiced during the first of four sessions before the show; Surya Bonaly, Nicole Bobek, Rudy Galindo and Tim Goebel also were on the ice at various times. Rudy landed seven triple-triple combination jumps in the practice. "I am really pushing myself," he says as he leaves the ice, drenched in sweat. "I can't do the quads, so I have to keep up in other ways."

5:02 p.m.

The zamboni takes a spin across the ice before the next practice session. A tabletop of scratches disappears under a thin coat of water.

5:11 p.m.

SASHA COHEN ARRIVES and takes a look at the ice. She runs into Johnny Weir, the 17-year-old world junior champion, and gives him a hug. Weir has been invited by Tom Collins to skate in the next four shows; he and his mother and his coach, Priscilla Hill, drove to Washington from their home in Newark, Del., this afternoon. Johnny is fighting his nerves; he knows this is how many of the tour's stars began, skating a couple of shows near their hometowns as up-and-coming teenagers.

5:14 p.m.

ROBIN WAGNER, Sarah Hughes' coach who has been sitting in the stands watching Sarah practice, tries to get backstage and finds her way blocked. An hour and a half earlier, there was an open passageway. "How did I do this before?" she asks Brian Klavano, the tour's performance director who is standing by the edge of the ice keeping an eye on practice. "You were younger and more agile," Klavano replies slyly. "But that was only an hour ago," protests Wagner. She proceeds to show Klavano just how carefully and gracefully she can hop over the gate.

5:20 p.m.

Tour security man Lou McClary, a former member of the Los Angeles police department who specializes in security for sports teams and this tour, holds a short meeting in the lower reaches of the MCI Center. He gathers the arena's operations manager, the supervisor of ushers and security personnel to talk about protecting the skaters. He mentions the names of stalkers who live in the area. He also talks about the autograph session that will occur after the show and where fans can and cannot go. This is not a special feature of the tour's visit to Washington; he does this before every show.

5:15 p.m.

Pairs practice begins. Isabelle Brasseur is a bit nervous about practicing the triple twist with partner Lloyd Eisler after giving him a black eye on that move in the show in Baltimore last night. They perform the move without incident today but decide to replace it with a hydrant lift in the show until Lloyd's eye heals.

5:23 p.m.

A worker runs a vacuum over the blue Champions on Ice rugs that lead from the dressing rooms to the ice. The show will start in a little more than two hours.

5:28 p.m.

Tim Goebel waits in a backstage hallway for Eric Lang to return to his physical therapy room to give Tim a massage and do some rehabilitative work on his aching right shoulder.

5:29 p.m.

SARAH HUGHES BUMPS into Tim Goebel. She is carrying her digital camera with pictures from her visit to the White House. "This is the Green Room," she tells Goebel. "This is Adams," she says, showing a photo of a portrait hanging on a wall. Next photo: "They have such beautiful chandeliers. I had to take a picture of this one." Next photo: "This is the state dining room. I called it the Gold Room. There's the Green Room, the Red Room, the Blue Room...why not the Gold Room?"

5:35 p.m.

Eric Lang returns and Tim Goebel disappears behind a closed door to receive treatment for his sore shoulder.

5:30 p.m.

Tour lighting director Dean Moyé has a brief conversation with Lloyd Eisler beside the ice. Dean wants to make sure Lloyd's eyesight is okay. He says it is. If there had been a problem, Dean could have changed the lighting, making the look on the ice brighter, to help Lloyd see better during his pairs number.

5:40 p.m.

As their practice ends, Isabelle Brasseur and "Uncle" Lloyd Eisler give Gabriella an "ice ride" around the rink. The little girl loves it.

5:41 p.m.

Other skaters take to the ice to practice: Dan Hollander, Michael Weiss, Viktor Petrenko, Elvis Stojko and Sasha Cohen. Because it was an unusual day with disrupted schedules, the skaters are taking practice time when they can fit it in rather than skating in the usual prescribed groups: men, ladies, pairs and dance.

5:55 p.m.

Isabelle Brasseur and Rocky Marval head to Catering with Gabriella, who is napping in her stroller. "Now she naps," Isabelle says, shaking her head.

5:56 p.m.

Margie Weiss is in charge of keeping two-year-old Christopher Weiss occupied while his father practices his jumps. Backstage, Christopher's eyes grow wide. "There's the zamboni," Christopher says to his grandmother. "I want to drive it."

5:57 p.m.

Evgeni Plushenko and Ukrainian acrobat Oleksiy Polishchuk find just enough room between the trucks and the equipment backstage to kick a soccer ball back and forth.

6:00 p.m.

*I*RINA SLUTSKAYA, who arrived at the MCI Center minutes earlier after getting caught in traffic, stretches and jogs backstage.

6:02 p.m.

Michelle Kwan steps onto the treadmill. The big clock put up hours earlier by backstage coordinator Jeff Wendt stares her in the face. She turns on her Discman, puts her earpieces in and begins walking.

6:05 p.m.

Lloyd Eisler does double-duty in Catering: he eats dinner while watching the second round of the Masters golf tournament on a television high above the buffet.

6:08 p.m.

His treatment over, Tim Goebel dashes to Catering for a second time. He fills a plate with a little bit of everything, not for himself but for Eric Lang, who gets so busy he has no time to escape for dinner. After grabbing something to drink, Goebel delivers the food to Lang's therapy room.

6:10 p.m.

The ice dancers practice last, but because schedules have changed for the day, there's an interloper. Irina Slutskaya has asked permission to join them because she missed her practice time. She's allowed, of course.

6:11 p.m.

Annie Mae Weiss leads Dan Hollander by the hand into Catering. "I'm her new boyfriend," Hollander says. He puts some roast beef on his plate and sits at a table with the Weiss family.

6:20 p.m.

Catering is getting crowded. Sarah and Amy Hughes walk in for dinner and squeeze their way past the packed tables to the buffet line.

6:29 p.m.

Michelle Kwan gets off the treadmill and begins stretching.

6:30 p.m.

Liz Punsalan and Jerod Swallow attend a John Hancock sponsors' gathering in a reception room at the MCI Center. Lou McClary gives a quick greeting to the sponsors, VIPs and their families, then encourages everyone to line up for an autograph session. It's a short event; Liz and Jerod are finished in 15 minutes.

6:33 p.m.

The dance practice ends and the zamboni returns to clean the ice for the show. Tour media coordinator Grant Rorvick is waiting for the two dance teams when they come off the ice. He has a Champions on Ice banner that needs to be signed by all the skaters to give to a sponsor, and they are the last. Victor Kraatz grabs a black Sharpie and signs his name; Peter Tchernyshev signs in blue.

6:35 p.m.

The doors open at the MCI Center. Fans begin to trickle in and find their seats. The skaters have disappeared backstage behind the black curtains that cover the entryway to the ice.

6:40 p.m.

Tim Goebel begins stretching on the blue mats beside the exercise equipment.

6:45 p.m.

Irina Slutskaya decides it's time to eat. She reaches over to a fruit plate held by Tom Collins and steals a cherry.

Slutskaya's roommate, Irina Grigorian, is in the dressing room putting on her makeup. She does not appear in the opening number, but she's beginning to get ready anyway.

6:50 p.m.

Michelle Kwan stops by athletic trainer Eric Lang's room to drop off a plate of dessert she picked up for him in Catering. He rewards her with a pre-show stretch.

6:51 p.m.

ℙHILIPPE CANDELORO ARRIVES at the MCI Center. He's had a busy day outdoors. The weather was warm and sunny, perfect for spring in Washington. "I walked around the city and Georgetown," he says. "I like Washington. It's a good city. Made by a French guy."

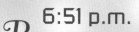

6:52 p.m.

Oleksiy Polishchuk and Evgeni Plushenko have put away the soccer ball and are now playing video hockey on one of the Sony PlayStations. Oleksiy's team is the United States, Evgeni's is Russia. At the moment, the USA is winning 5–2. "Yeah, as always," shouts Rudy Galindo, who is laughing and stretching on the mats next to the PlayStations with his pal Nicole Bobek.

6:53 p.m.

Rudy Galindo turns over onto his back on the mats. "Is that asbestos?" he asks no one in particular, looking up at the backstage ceiling. Jerod Swallow, who is standing near the mats, looks up. "The building's too new," Jerod replies. "It's some kind of fire retardant." Satisfied, Rudy goes back to stretching.

6:55 p.m.

Viktor Petrenko has made it to the exercise equipment but only to sit on it and make cell phone calls. "First I talk, later I work out," he says with a wry smile.

7:00 p.m.

NICOLE BOBEK and Irina Slutskaya look like they are stretching beside the exercise equipment at Petrenko's feet, but they're not. They are spread out on their stomachs, their feet at opposite ends of the mats, their heads together, examining their nails. Sarah Hughes jogs by. She can't help but notice them. "What are you doing?" she yells out, making a U-turn and jogging toward them. "We're looking at our nails," Bobek says. Sarah leans over and throws her hands into the mix for a moment of analysis, then turns around and jogs off.

7:07 p.m.

IN THE HALLWAY to the dressing rooms, there is a scene that is causing all passing skaters to turn and stare: Surya Bonaly's new skate boots are cooking at 250 degrees in a toaster oven. Bonaly and her mother are meeting with Mike Cunningham, a skate specialist who lives in the Washington area, so Surya can be fitted for new boots that are molded to the feet when they're warm. "Walk around in them for a few minutes," Cunningham says, sounding like a shoe salesman at Nordstrom. Surya likes the boots, but she won't wear them tonight; the blades are not yet attached.

7:10 p.m.

JON DREW, the tour's music director and announcer, charges down the hallway past Surya and the toaster oven. "Half hour!" he yells. The show is scheduled to start at 7:30, but no show ever starts on time. The crew and staff always give the audience a 10- to 15-minute grace period to find their seats and get settled. It's Drew's job to count down the time for the skaters, who are living in a vacuum backstage. Most do not wear watches when they skate so they easily lose track of time. Drew is their human timepiece, walking toward the skaters at the exercise equipment, in the dressing room, in the hallways, performing his duties like a latter-day Paul Revere: "Half hour!" he shouts again. "Half hour!"

7:22 p.m.

Tim Goebel is still stretching on the mats. Jerod Swallow's legs are churning on the StairMaster.

7:25 p.m.

Jon Drew's voice echoes down the hall. "Make that 15, guys. Fifteen minutes!"

7:26 p.m.

Philippe Candeloro and acrobat Vladimir Besedin are playing ping-pong as Drew walks by. Candeloro is dressed in casual clothes. His skates and his outfit for the show's opening number are back in the dressing room. He is in no hurry. "This is how I warm up," he says with a mischievous smile. Vladimir also is in no rush, but unlike Philippe, he's not in the opening number.

7:32 p.m.

Jon Drew walks to the spot where he will stand all evening, at ice level beside the skaters' entrance to the ice. "Welcome to John Hancock Champions on Ice…." he says into the microphone. This is the opening line he delivers every night. The show is still several minutes from beginning.

7:35 p.m.

As most skaters are getting into their costumes and putting on their makeup for the opening, Evgeni Plushenko dashes out of Catering in his workout clothes carrying a plate of roast beef.

7:36 p.m.

Jon Drew is backstage again. "Five minutes!" Tim Goebel knows this is his cue. He goes to the dressing room to change from his workout clothes to his blue and black outfit for the opening number.

7:38 p.m.

Naomi Lang is lined up in a red dress with black highlights, standing in the hallway talking to Rocky Marval and Liz DeSevo, her agents. They ask how she is feeling; she is one of the skaters with a cold. "I don't feel anything," Naomi says, shrugging. "I took Contac." "Contac?" Rocky asks. "They still have that?"

. . . .

7:39 p.m.

Ready for the opening number, Isabelle Brasseur trudges down the hallway wearing pink and purple skate guards, pushing a sleeping Gabriella in a stroller. She leaves the stroller with her husband, Rocky Marval. "We'll be here when you get back," Rocky says to his wife.

7:40 p.m.

Lloyd Eisler comes down the hallway and walks up to Isabelle and family. He peeks into the stroller. "Still snoozing," he says.

7:41 p.m.

*T*OUR MANAGER Michael Collins pops out of his backstage office, looking for Victor Kraatz. He wants to hand Victor his new work visa so he can put it with his belongings in the dressing room. As the skaters begin to line up in the hallway with the show about to start, Michael asks Shae-Lynn Bourne where her partner is. Shae-Lynn smiles. "I don't know, but I'm bound to see him. Like in a minute or two."

7:42 p.m.

Michael Weiss and Elvis Stojko emerge from the locker room and walk down the hallway toward the other skaters. Victor Kraatz reports for duty right behind them and joins Shae-Lynn in the line-up. "I kind of thought I'd see him," Shae-Lynn says with a laugh.

. . . .

7:43 p.m.

Jon Drew walks back to his perch beside the ice: "The show will begin in one minute!" There is scattered applause from the crowd of 15,000. The skaters are stretched in a long, snaking line beginning at the black-draped chute that leads to the ice. Everyone is shaking an arm or a leg; that qualifies as last-minute tour exercise. Michelle Kwan, dressed in purple and black, clumps down the hallway in her skates to join the group, giving her nose one last swipe with a tissue. Like Sarah Hughes, Sasha Cohen and Naomi Lang, she is fighting a cold. And Michelle learned long ago that there are no sick days in this line of work.

7:44 p.m.

The tour's opening music, John Williams' 2002 Olympic theme, "Call of the Champions," booms from the 20,000-pound sound system hanging over center ice in the darkened MCI Center. This is the "Citius, Altius, Fortius" music from the Salt Lake City Games. Spotlights flood the ice and pan the crowd, washing everyone and everything with the Olympic rings. Although this is already the ninth show of 93, the air of anticipation among the spectators who paid up to $65 a seat is matched by that of the athletes waiting anxiously in the dark down below. Joining them beside the ice is production manager Paul Hendrickson — showered, dressed up and medicated — who has emerged from backstage to make sure everything inside the arena is in working order.

7:45 p.m.

*T*HE STRAINS OF the famous Olympic theme music "Bugler's Dream" resound in the arena.

Jon Drew's voice reaches over the music: "Tom Collins presents the 2002 tour of Champions on Ice." Lloyd Eisler and Isabelle Brasseur, clustered with their colleagues at the entrance to the ice, take off their skate guards and glide into position at center ice, still invisible in the darkness. "Brasseur and Eisler!" Jon Drew intones. The spotlights come on, and Isabelle is in the air, spinning over Lloyd's head. The show has begun.

7:46 p.m.

Out they come, one skater after another, the roar of the crowd building as each new name is called. Nicole Bobek charges onto the ice in bright blue, finishing with the splits as the next skater, her best friend Rudy Galindo, opens with a set of splits of his own.

7:49 p.m.

Philippe Candeloro, all dressed up with time to spare, as it turns out, twists open one of the 30 bottles of water sitting on a table beside the ice for the skaters; he takes a sip as Naomi Lang and Peter Tchernyshev hydroblade across the ice. In a moment, when Jon Drew calls his name, the spotlight will leave the dancers and find Candeloro.

7:50 p.m.

Philippe Candeloro reaches into the crowd and kisses his first woman of the evening. It will not be his last. He does not take off his shirt, but there's still plenty of time for that. This, after all, is only the opening number.

7:51 p.m.

As the introductions continue on the ice, Nicole Bobek races backstage to Roger Bathurst's wardrobe room. He is waiting there to help her make the quick change to her costume for her *Moulin Rouge* number. Nicole is the show's first individual performer and cannot participate in the rest of the group opening because she has to be ready for her number the moment the other skaters leave the ice.

7:52 p.m.

*M*ichael Weiss, skating before his hometown crowd, effortlessly lands the toughest jump anyone tries in the opening, a triple lutz.

7:53 p.m.

As Viktor Petrenko dances to the familiar words and beat of "All Star" on the ice, Michelle Kwan and Evgeni Plushenko, standing side by side waiting their turn in the pitch-black chute to the ice, do a little dance of their own, together.

7:54 p.m.

Michelle Kwan swirls around the ice for a moment in the darkness as Elvis Stojko performs in the spotlight. When Elvis finishes, Michelle races to center ice as the spotlights find her. The announcement comes next: "Michelle Kwan!" The audience cheers loudly and cameras flash throughout the arena as the music changes to George Harrison's "Here Comes the Sun." Michelle performs a flying camel spin, then races around the ice to pick up speed for her change-of-edge spiral, before reaching her arm out to present the next skater: "Timothy Goebel!"

7:57 p.m.

Tim Goebel hands off to Irina Slutskaya who makes way for Evgeni Plushenko. There is only one skater remaining in the dark entry area. "Sarah Hughes!" says Jon Drew, and the audience roars. "The World's Greatest" plays as Sarah lands a triple loop, then is joined by the rest of the skaters for a short group number, a wave and a mad dash for the skate guards that are strewn throughout the dark entryway.

7:58 p.m.

Nicole Bobek takes the ice for her solo. Sarah Hughes puts on a warm-up jacket over her red dress and stands with Surya Bonaly and Philippe Candeloro by the black curtains in the entryway. She watches a few moments of Nicole's number before heading backstage to change into casual clothes for the nearly two-hour wait before she skates again.

8:00 p.m.

*T*IM GOEBEL has a long wait as well, about an hour and a half, so he puts his workout clothes back on and begins a regimen of stretching and pilates.

8:03 p.m.

*A*LTHOUGH ISABELLE BRASSEUR and Lloyd Eisler don't perform until the end of the first act, they have no time to waste backstage. Isabelle goes into Eric Lang's small room to receive treatment on her legs, which bother her because of a heart condition. As Eric does his work, Lloyd joins them and draws a goatee on Isabelle's face with an eyebrow pencil. They are performing a number that has her playing a man and him, a woman, so after Lloyd takes care of Isabelle, he spends the rest of his time turning himself into a dress-wearing, wig-modeling, high-heeled, meticulously made-up young lady.

8:08 p.m.

Philippe Candeloro takes the ice for his "Wild Wild West" program, bringing a clothes hamper onto the ice with him. Much of what he is wearing at the beginning of his number will end up in or near the hamper by the end of the program.

8:09 p.m.

Philippe picks out a woman in the audience and hugs and kisses her. She slaps him on the rear end.

8:10 p.m.

Philippe's hat, vest, outer pants and shirt all come off in the same minute.

8:11 p.m.

Philippe kisses a different woman, his third of the evening.

8:12 p.m.

His gun-slinging program finished, Philippe gathers all his belongings — this takes a minute — and leaves the ice.

8:13 p.m.

Liz Punsalan and Jerod Swallow's intricate and melancholy performance of "Because" and "One Is the Loneliest Number" dramatically changes the mood in the arena. Sarah Hughes pops out from behind the curtains to sit in a row of folding chairs beside the ice and watch with her mother Amy.

8:15 p.m.

Making the rounds of all the backstage games, Evgeni Plushenko is now at the ping-pong table with Oleksiy Polishchuk.

8:20 p.m.

As Dan Hollander performs as Mrs. Doubtfire on the ice, Shae-Lynn Bourne and Victor Kraatz, already in costume but wearing warm-up jackets, go through an intense, dry-land, street-shoes version of their performance, which is still nearly an hour away. They are going about their work beside one of the huge trucks in the loading area; it's the only place they can find the room to train.

8:27 p.m.

SASHA COHEN LEAVES the ice after her performance of "Hernando's Hideaway." Catching her breath as she grabs a water bottle and reaches for her skate guards, she turns to watch Michael Weiss stand on his head on the ice, then do a back flip, just as his father taught him to do.

8:32 p.m.

With Surya Bonaly on the ice doing more back flips and the closing number an hour and a half away, Liz Punsalan climbs on the elliptical trainer for her daily workout while her husband gets his workout on one of the PlayStations, choosing a game called "Grand Theft Auto." Elvis Stojko is sitting at the PlayStation next door, playing "Dark Cloud," which requires almost as much intensity as a triple axel. Peter Tchernyshev is watching nearby. A ping-pong ball bounces toward him. He tosses it back to the outstretched hands of Philippe Candeloro, who has returned to the table for another game.

8:35 p.m.

Rudy Galindo appears for his Village People medley in his "In the Navy" shirt, which is nice and clean thanks to Roger Bathurst's morning laundry duty. All the tour's outfits are washable; there is no time for dry-cleaning on this 85-city tour. Within a minute, Rudy has half the audience joining him for "Y-M-C-A," his old stand-by.

8:40 p.m.

Isabelle Brasseur, in goatee, T-shirt, denim and black skates, "throws" Lloyd Eisler across the ice. He lands a single axel. The crowd loves it.

8:42 p.m.

Isabelle and Lloyd trudge through the black curtains. "My wig is falling off," Lloyd complains.

8:43 p.m.

Intermission begins, but few take a break backstage. The workouts and stretching continue. But Philippe Candeloro, who is finished until the finale, isn't working out. He's taking a short nap in the dressing room.

8:45 p.m.

Irina Grigorian stands by the chute to the ice, twirling a hula hoop, all dressed up and ready to go.

8:47 p.m.

Young Johnny Weir silently paces outside the chute to the ice; he's first to skate in the second act.

8:49 p.m.

Michelle Kwan, wearing workout clothes, finds a quiet place backstage to stretch.

8:50 p.m.

Isabelle Brasseur wipes off her makeup. She takes Gabriella to the exercise area where she lifts some weights while her daughter watches a "Teletubbies" video on a DVD player.

8:55 p.m.

Shae-Lynn Bourne and Victor Kraatz are stretching backstage.

8:58 p.m.

Tim Goebel hops on the StairMaster for a quick workout.

9:00 p.m.

ERIC LANG TAKES a moment away from his serious work to replenish his candy drawer. Frequent visitors to the drawer include Sasha Cohen, Rudy Galindo, Nicole Bobek, Liz Punsalan, Jerod Swallow, Surya Bonaly, Tim Goebel, Shae-Lynn Bourne, Sarah Hughes and even Tom Collins, he reports.

9:01 p.m.

Awake after his cat nap, Philippe Candeloro joins Evgeni Plushenko at the ping-pong table. After the game, Candeloro reports: "He killed me."

9:02 p.m.

Jon Drew flips the switch on his microphone to start the second act. "He's the 2001 junior world champion… Johnny Weir." As Weir performs "Songs from a Secret Garden," his exhibition number from last season, a half-dozen skaters file through the curtain to watch: Nicole Bobek, Peter Tchernyshev and Sasha Cohen among them. Bobek is nervous for him. "I remember when I did this years ago in Chicago, skating in my hometown with the tour for the first time," she says. "All the skaters came out like this to watch me. I got so nervous I think I fell on everything." Johnny Weir has a much better opening night than Bobek did; he falls on his triple lutz but lands three more triples as well as a double axel. When he finishes, Bobek applauds.

9:09 p.m.

IRINA GRIGORIAN is spinning eight hula hoops from head to toe while on skates. Needless to say, she tries no triple jumps.

9:11 p.m.

Practice time finally ends for Shae-Lynn Bourne and Victor Kraatz as they glide onto the ice for their performance of "Sadeness."

9:16 p.m.

While acrobats Oleksiy Polishchuk and Vladimir Besedin, both in white tutus, become the most unlikely ballerinas ever to perform to *Swan Lake*, Tim Goebel runs in place backstage.

9:19 p.m.

In her father's arms beside the ice, Annie Mae Weiss watches Elvis Stojko perform. As Elvis finishes, Annie Mae greets him with a high-five.

9:22 p.m.

An inveterate program-watcher when he's not napping or playing ping-pong, Philippe Candeloro takes in Tim Goebel's Paul McCartney number, nodding his head approvingly as he watches. Goebel isn't trying the quad these days because it's not an easy jump to complete successfully with no on-ice warm-up and under show lighting. But he does land four triple jumps and a double axel.

9:27 p.m.

Irina Slutskaya, a most unlikely Western cowgirl to "Cotton-Eyed Joe," waits her turn in the entryway as Tim Goebel finishes. "I'm scared," she says. "Of what?" she is asked. "Of my performance. I am so tired. I don't know if I can jump at all."

9:28 p.m.

"The new world champion… Irina Slutskaya." Just hearing those words thrills Irina. "I live for this," she says. "They can never take this away from me." She pumps her fist and out she goes.

9:30 p.m.

Shae-Lynn Bourne is on the mats in the exercise area, stretching after her performance. She also works on a few handstands with the help of acrobat Oleksiy Polishchuk. "If I fall," she says, "he catches my legs."

9:31 p.m.

Waiting for Sarah Hughes to change in the dressing room, Robin Wagner, Sarah's coach, sits on a folding chair in the hallway, leafing through fashion magazines. She is looking for ideas for next season for Sarah: new looks, styles, clothes. "Anything that hits me," she says. "Colors, ideas, trends for this year."

9:32 p.m.

As VIKTOR PETRENKO'S unmistakable music — "Who Let the Dogs Out" — wafts backstage, Michelle Kwan marches down the hallway, her eyes straight ahead, heading for the ice. Irina Slutskaya passes Michelle in the hallway, her work already completed. "I did the triple loop!" Irina tells Nicole Bobek and Rudy Galindo, who are sitting on the floor outside the men's dressing room, giggling together. They look up. "I landed everything," Irina says. "I'm so happy." Nicole and Rudy pat Irina on the legs as she walks by. "Way to go!" Nicole yells.

9:34 p.m.

Viktor Petrenko skates around a corner of the ice with a fluffy dog puppet attached to his arm — and hears fans barking at him. He thinks that's a little strange. Then again, he's the first man in skating history to land a double axel with a dog puppet attached to his arm.

9:36 p.m.

"America's own…" That's all Jon Drew has to say. The audience knows who's next. He finishes his line anyway: "Michelle Kwan!"

9:40 p.m.

As Michelle Kwan lands the third of her four perfect jumps in the emotional "Fields of Gold," Sarah Hughes emerges from the curtains to watch while tugging at the zipper in the back of her white dress.

9:41 p.m.

The audience gives Michelle the first standing ovation of the evening. All zipped up, Sarah Hughes practices waltz jumps on the rug beside the ice in the darkness — with her skate guards still on.

9:43 p.m.

Evgeni Plushenko is next, performing his *Carmen* Olympic long program as Sarah Hughes continues her off-ice jumping. She stops to watch Plushenko's flawless triple lutz. "A couple triple lutzes like that and I'll be all set," she says.

9:48 p.m.

"The new Olympic champion..." Sarah Hughes is greeted with an overwhelming roar. She lands her one and only triple lutz with ease in her brand new "I'll Never Say Goodbye" program.

9:49 p.m.

Michelle Kwan and Irina Slutskaya step out from behind the backstage curtain, now both dressed in red, white and blue for the finale. They watch Sarah Hughes for a moment, then step back behind the curtain.

9:50 p.m.

The skaters begin to gather for the finale on the rug beside the ice as Sarah ends with a precarious triple loop. "Dig it out," Tim Goebel says as he watches. She does. "Good." He turns back to the other skaters assembled around him. "There's been a lot of that tonight," he says with a smile.

9:51 p.m.

Sarah Hughes' performance ends. She has landed four triple jumps and a double axel. The audience rises to its feet for the second time in 10 minutes. Another standing ovation.

9:52 p.m.

"Ladies and gentlemen," Jon Drew says, "please join your Champions on Ice as we honor America." Sarah dashes through the curtain to jump into the red, white and blue dress Robin Wagner is holding in the quick-change room backstage. On the ice, the first of the skaters files out for the finale, then the strains of Jimi Hendrix's "The Star-Spangled Banner" resound throughout the arena.

9:53 p.m.

*T*HERE ARE RUSSIANS dressed in red, white
and blue; Canadians in red, white and blue; French
skaters in red, white and blue. What's going on here?
It so happens that the Russian and French flags are
red, white and blue, but that's merely a coincidence,
because all the Champions on Ice skaters are
celebrating the United States for the next seven
minutes in the tour's stirring tribute to September 11.

9:54 p.m.

Tim Goebel glides into the spotlight in a spread
eagle to Ray Charles' "America the Beautiful" as
Michelle Kwan takes off her skate guards and
Sarah Hughes re-emerges next to her on the rug
at the edge of the ice.

9:56 p.m.

The music has changed
to the "Battle Hymn of
the Republic," and Sarah
Hughes comes flying
back to the ice to perform
a falling leaf, then a
combination spin.

9:58 p.m.

Michelle Kwan is last onto the ice,
landing a triple toe loop as the
"Battle Hymn of the Republic"
soars to its rousing conclusion.
The spotlights find Michelle in the
middle of the ice just as the music
reaches its heart-pounding
crescendo. Always one to try to
block out the crowd to do her job
on the ice, Michelle can't help it
this time. She gets goose bumps.

9:59 p.m.

As the music ends, the U.S. flags unfurl from the rafters, all four flying the proper way thanks to tour production manager Paul Hendrickson's attention to detail 10 hours earlier. Dozens of fireworks pop at the end of the wires hanging from the lighting trusses. The audience rises to its feet again. It's the Fourth of July in April.

10:00 p.m.

*T*HE SKATERS WAVE. The arena goes dark. The show is over; the skaters' mad dash off the ice begins. As they grab their skate guards and funnel through the chute backstage, an autograph seeker holds a program above Sarah Hughes' head. She notices, reaches up and quickly signs it for the fan.

10:05 p.m.

It's standing room only in the dressing rooms. Tim Goebel heads to the shower. So does Philippe Candeloro. Dan Hollander and Michael Weiss grab a plate and fill it with the vegetable lasagna the caterer has put in both dressing rooms. Dan eats with a knife because there aren't enough forks.

10:06 p.m.

The tour's quality control/second-guessing department is already hard at work. Tom Collins thinks the fireworks went off a few seconds too early. He finds performance director Brian Klavano and pyrotechnician Ray Seymour, the man who pushes the button to set off the display, to ask them what they thought. They tell him everything was perfect. Tom takes their word for it, kind of. He plans to watch closely during tomorrow's finale.

10:07 p.m.

As the skaters get dressed, nearly 200 spectators stream downstairs to a secure roped-off area beside the trucks for the tour's nightly autograph, photo and handshake session. These fans received special backstage passes for the occasion. Lou McClary, the former policeman, watches keenly as the spectators file in.

10:12 p.m.

McClary introduces Johnny Weir to the fans, kicking off the evening's "Meet and Greet" with the skaters. "Ladies and gentlemen, Johnny opened the second half of our show," McClary announces. Johnny works his way slowly down the line, with the fans on one side of a rope and the skaters on the other. He has never signed so many autographs in his life.

10:14 p.m.

The skaters emerge one by one from the dressing room, some with wet hair, to begin their autograph duties on the way to the bus. Many carry their own Sharpie pens to make the job simpler.

10:15 p.m.

His day's work complete, tour production manager Paul Hendrickson steps into the fresh evening air outside the MCI Center for the four-block walk to the crew hotel, the Grand Hyatt. It's a rare night indeed when the crew gets to sleep in a bed that's not traveling at 60 mph. Because there is a second show in Washington tomorrow afternoon, the crew stays put tonight and does not have to sleep on the bus. Paul checks into the hotel, takes a shower, takes his medicine and is asleep within 45 minutes.

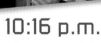

10:16 p.m.

Always one of the first skaters out of the dressing room, Shae-Lynn Bourne hits the autograph line.

10:20 p.m.

Sasha Cohen sits alone on a blue case backstage, drinking a cup of tea to soothe her sore throat before heading to the line of spectators.

10:24 p.m.

Michelle Kwan makes the long, slow march down the line, posing for at least two dozen pictures, signing at least 50 autographs.

10:28 p.m.

Bringing up the rear, Sarah Hughes dives into her "Meet and Greet" duties.

10:30 p.m.

Shae-Lynn Bourne reaches the bus. She gets on and sees announcer Jon Drew. They begin chatting about the show.

10:36 p.m.

DAN HOLLANDER works his way down the line, helping fans find his picture in the program. Few recognize him without his dress and wig.

10:44 p.m.

Oleksiy Polishchuk, the little acrobat, jokes with fans about his partner Vladimir Besedin, the big guy. "He drops me every night."

10:47 p.m.

THE BUS IS FILLING up with skaters and staff members pulling skate bags and carrying briefcases. In the loading dock, several straggling skaters continue to work the line. Lou McClary stands near Sarah Hughes, keeping an eye on the fans, just doing his job.

10:53 p.m.

Sarah Hughes is still signing, talking and smiling for pictures. Tom Collins sidles over to Sarah and her mother, Amy, who is doing her share of chatting with fans who want to meet "Sarah's mom." Tom shakes his head in mock anger: "We need a crane to pick Sarah up and get her out of here."

10:55 p.m.

Sarah Hughes reaches the last fan. After one final autograph, she climbs aboard the tour bus.

10:56 p.m.

The bus chugs up the ramp and out of the MCI Center. Several fans stand on the sidewalk holding signs. "Wave to your fans," Tom Collins reminds the skaters. They follow his orders.

11:00 p.m.

*T*RAINER ERIC LANG makes the rounds on the bus to see if anyone needs his help. "The iceman cometh," he says. He dispenses a few bags of ice and is satisfied that everyone is healthy enough to skate another day.

11:11 p.m.

Bus driver Rich Banas has figured out a new, more direct way back to the Four Seasons. Tom Collins notices and applauds.

11:13 p.m.

*T*HE BUS PULLS UP on Pennsylvania Avenue near the hotel. Tom Collins, Lou McClary and Rich Banas immediately hop onto the sidewalk and race each other to see how quickly they can pull the skaters' bags out of the luggage hold and put them on the sidewalk. Their game, a daily ritual on tour, amuses a few passers-by. The skaters, on the other hand, have come to expect this. They barely pay attention.

11:16 p.m.

Evgeni Plushenko walks through the lobby and hops into an elevator crowded with colleagues to head to his room.

11:18 p.m.

Sarah Hughes and Sasha Cohen, each pulling a travel bag on wheels, jump into an elevator together.

11:20 p.m.

*B*ack in the lobby, an elevator door opens and Evgeni Plushenko pops out. "Key doesn't work," he says, shrugging, walking to the front desk. He soon returns with another one.

11:25 p.m.

In her room, Irina Slutskaya takes off her makeup, takes a shower, brushes her teeth and does her nails.

11:30 p.m.

Robin Wagner and her husband, Jerry Grossman, order cheeseburgers in the Four Seasons lobby bar.

Isabelle Brasseur falls asleep in her hotel room with Gabriella in her arms.

11:35 p.m.

Michelle Kwan meets tour publicity man Grant Rorvick for a late snack in the lobby bar.

11:42 p.m.

Tour manager Michael Collins swipes a french fry off Robin Wagner's plate as he walks past her table to join his father for a late-night business meeting at another table.

11:43 p.m.

There's a knock at the door in the room of the two Irinas, Slutskaya and Grigorian. Evgeni Plushenko and Oleksiy Polishchuk want to come in to use Irina Grigorian's computer to quickly check their e-mail. The Irinas invite them in.

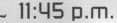

11:45 p.m.

*T*IM GOEBEL, Shae-Lynn Bourne, Naomi Lang, Philippe Candeloro and Vladimir Besedin, accompanied by friends who attended the show, push several tables together in the lobby bar at the Four Seasons. "We pretty much take over the lobby bar in every hotel we're in," says Goebel, who has ordered the fried goat cheese. "Everyone still has a lot of energy in the hour after the show," says Bourne.

11:50 p.m.

In her room, Sarah Hughes signs on to the Internet on her laptop. Amy Hughes goes to the lobby bar to join Robin Wagner and her husband.

11:47 p.m.

A woman comes by to say hello to the group. Philippe Candeloro ends up giving her a hug and a kiss. She's the fourth woman he has kissed tonight.

11:55 p.m.

Evgeni Plushenko and Oleksiy Polishchuk leave the room of Irina and Irina. Irina Grigorian takes a bubble bath. Irina Slutskaya goes to sleep. "It's been a long day," she says to herself.

12:00 midnight

*L*IZ PUNSALAN and Jerod Swallow turn out the lights in their room and go to sleep.

Tom and Michael Collins do a post-mortem on the show at their table in the bar. Once again, everything came together. "It doesn't get much better than this," Michael says. "Nine shows down," says Tom, to which Michael adds, "Only 84 to go."

1 Skaters with Siegfried and Roy; 2 Michelle Kwan and her dog, Tofu; 3 Young fans; 4 Irina Slutskaya and Tim Goebel; 5 Tom; 6 Katarina Witt and Sabine Baess, 1981; 7 Opening of Rockefeller Center rink, 2000.

8 Gwendal Peizerat and Laurent Tobel at the Mall of America;
9 Paul Duchesnay; **10** Viktor Petrenko and his coach, Galina;
11 Tom and skaters in Las Vegas; **12** Surya Bonaly;
13 Michelle Kwan and Irina Slutskaya.

14 Kristi Yamaguchi, Michael Collins and Peggy Fleming, 1994;
15 Brian Boitano, Tom and Brian Orser, 1988.

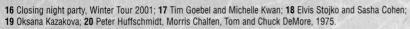

16 Closing night party, Winter Tour 2001; **17** Tim Goebel and Michelle Kwan; **18** Elvis Stojko and Sasha Cohen; **19** Oksana Kazakova; **20** Peter Huffschmidt, Morris Chalfen, Tom and Chuck DeMore, 1975.

21 Christopher Dean; **22** Dick Button, Michelle Kwan, Tom and Patricia Michael; **23** Michael Seibert and Lisa Marie Allen; **24** Grant Rorvick.

25 Rocky Marval, Isabelle Brasseur and daughter Gabriella; **26** Nancy Kerrigan and son Matthew; **27** Sarah Hughes turns 17; **28** Costume designer fitting Sarah; **29** Vladimir Besedin and daughter; **30** Irina Slutskaya and Michelle Kwan; **31** Viktor and Nina Petrenko's wedding reception, 1992; **32** Oksana Kazakova; **33** Shae-Lynn Bourne and Tom.

Index

Credits

2002 CHAMPIONS ON ICE STAFF AND CREW

Tom Collins . . . . *Executive Producer*
Don Watson . . . . *Executive Vice President*
Sarah Kawahara . . . *Director of Staging/Choreography*
David Sutton . . . . *General Manager*
Michael Collins . . . . *Tour Manager*
Marty Collins . . . . *Tour Coordinator*
Bill Lee . . . . *Vice President/Marketing*
Sandy Reed . . . . *Executive Coordinator*
Pat Gale . . . . *Creative Director*
Lynn Plage . . . . *Director of Media Relations*
Noel Watson . . . . *Vice President/Sales and eBusiness*
Brian M. Klavano . . . . *Performance Director*
Paul Hendrickson . . . . *Production Manager*
Jon Drew . . . . *Music Director/Announcer*
Grant Rorvick . . . . *Media Coordinator*
Elaine DeMore . . . . *U.S.F.S.A. Representative*
Eric Lang . . . . *Physical Therapist*
Dean Moyé . . . . *Lighting Director*
Miles Bryant . . . . *Original Music*
Jeff Wendt . . . . *Backstage Coordinator*
Rob Lindsay . . . . *Audio Engineer*

Paul Tillman . . . . *Audio Engineer*
Marilyn Lowey . . . . *Lighting Designer*
Mike Lehrman . . . . *Lighting Crew Chief*
Jim Ellis . . . . *Lighting Technician*
Brian M. Hijos . . . . *Lighting Technician*
Nelson Meeks . . . . *Lighting Technician*
Chad Williams . . . . *Lighting Technician*
Ray Seymour . . . . *Pyrotechnican*
Roger Bathurst . . . . *Wardrobe Supervisor*
Mark Collins . . . . *Merchandising Director*
Rich Banas . . . . *Bus Driver*
Paul Braundel . . . . *Bus Driver*
Danny Love . . . . *Bus Driver*
David Coppersmith . . . . *Truck Driver*
Steve Dodge . . . . *Truck Driver*
Dale Hickingbottom . . . . *Truck Driver*
Jeff Lawrence . . . . *Truck Driver*
Jim Means . . . . *Truck Driver*
Mike Reed . . . . *Truck Driver*
Lou McClary . . . . *Security Director*

PHOTO CREDITS

Many of figure skating's most accomplished photographers contributed to *Champions on Ice*:

Heinz Kluetmeier shot most of the recent performance photos and much of the backstage activity;

Isabelle Brasseur provided a skater's-eye view of life on tour both backstage and away from the rink;

Paul and Michelle Harvath enhanced the book with their on-ice skater portraits and annual group photos;

Roy Blakey documented the tour's history by photographing complete sets of yearly program covers, backstage passes, jackets and other crested items.

Champions on Ice, the Collins family and the World Figure Skating Museum contributed images from their collections.

Additional photos by: Dave Black, Ingrid Butt, Gerard Chataigneau, Karen Cover, Marc Evon, Arnie Feder, Frank Heaney, Harry Langdon, Eileen Langsley, Victoria Newman, Don Shelley, Keith A. Vendouem, Gerri Waldert and the White House.

Acknowledgements

A PROJECT LIKE THIS could not have been accomplished without the assistance of many people. Thank you, first and foremost, to Tom Collins and the Collins family: Jane, Michael, Mark, Marty and Butch. They were especially generous with their time and ideas, and they couldn't have been more accommodating in opening up their tour to me.

Thanks, also, to the cast, staff and crew of Champions on Ice, past and present, for their time and effort on my behalf. I would like to especially mention Paul Hendrickson, Dean Moyé, Brian Klavano, Lou McClary, Grant Rorvick, Sandy Reed, Pat Gale and Don and Noel Watson. Lynn Plage, the "champion off ice," deserves special thanks for her untiring help. And thank you to Isabelle Brasseur, a pairs skater with a penchant for shooting the perfect backstage photo.

In Toronto, editor Dan Diamond saw this project through from beginning to end — and kept his sense of humor throughout. Without him, there would be no book. Thanks also to Paul Bontje, Ralph Dinger, James Duplacey, Patricia MacDonald, Eric Zweig and Jonathan Zweig from his office.

The hard-working people at PageWave Graphics created this beautiful book. Thank you to Joseph Gisini, who took my words and brought them to life. Thanks also to Daniella Zanchetta, who now knows more about skating than most skaters, and Andrew Smith and Kevin Cockburn.

Thanks also to the people at Embassy Stafford — Kevin Barry, Peter Brugger, Tuan Doan, Joe Fonseca and Chris Whalen — who turned the book from black-and-white to color.

It was a delight to have the opportunity to work with photographer Heinz Kluetmeier. I have been a fan of his for more than two decades, since his magnificent picture of the 1980 U.S. hockey team's upset of the Soviets graced the cover of *Sports Illustrated*. And thanks to a new generation of photographers, symbolized by Jennie and Leslie Backoff.

Back in the writing and reporting department, I want to thank several people who worked behind the scenes to help me, including Linda Leaver, Jean Hall, Shep Goldberg, John Day, Roy Blakey, Bob Dunlop, Jill Lieber and Amy Brennan Swaak. Lori Nichol deserves a special thank you for giving me numerous suggestions for the book, including the idea to chronicle "A Day in the Life" of the tour.

I want to close by thanking my wonderful family for seeing me through another book project: Kate, Tom, Brad, Jennie and Leslie Backoff; Jim, Angela, Henry and Kathryn Brennan; Amy, Derrick and Peter Swaak. My Dad was with me all the way, as always, and my Mom was too, just in a different way.

— Christine Brennan

A Message from Tom Collins

*T*HIS BOOK, the story of Champions on Ice, has been a dream of mine for a long time. Preparing for it brought back so many wonderful memories of 25 seasons of skating shows. I hope you get as much pleasure reading these memories as I had living them.

I have many people to thank:

First and foremost, to my late sister Marty, who was my inspiration and started me on this journey. You are the reason I am where I am today. Thank you.

For my wife Jane and my three sons, Mike, Mark, and Marty: For years and years, I was away for many months at a time and yet you were always there waiting for me with open arms. I can't thank you enough for that — and for everything.

To Butch, for being Butch, my brother.

Thank you to my late brother Harris for his creativity and unwavering support. You were my guiding light.

Thanks to Morris Chalfen, the person who came up with the idea to bring this tour to North America in 1969.

To Sandy Reed, my executive assistant, thank you for your dedication and for putting up with me for all these years.

A special thank you to my loyal friends and colleagues Don and Noel Watson, David Sutton, Shep Goldberg, Michael Rosenberg, Paul Hendrickson, Marilyn Lowey and Pat Gale for their tireless efforts.

Many people were generous with their time and insights throughout my career. I would particularly like to thank Roger Bathurst, Elaine and Chuck DeMore, Jon Drew, Richard Feldstein, Bud Freeman, Al Grant, Elliot Harris, Eric Lang, Lou McClary, Dale Mitch, Dean Moyé, Bill Wirtz, and Susan Zepkin. I also want to thank the International Skating Union, United States Figure Skating Association and Skate Canada.

Thank you to the newer members of our company who are helping continue the Champions on Ice tradition: Sarah Kawahara, Brian Klavano, Grant Rorvick, and Pete Menefee. *Encore!*

For their help in shaping the content of the shows and this book, I would like to thank all of the skaters who have appeared in Champions on Ice. Without the skaters I would not have lived my dream.

Thanks to Christine Brennan for dedicating herself to the writing of a fair, honest and innovative book. It was my pleasure to work with her.

Thanks to Lynn Plage for always being there, with energy and enthusiasm. She is a magnificent publicist.

And thanks to the Toronto gang, the people who made this book come to life: Dan Diamond, the folks at PageWave Graphics and Embassy Stafford and special guest star Lori Nichol.

You've all been a very special part of my life. Thanks to everyone for sharing my 25-year road trip.

I hope you've enjoyed the show.